OPERATION CAR WASH

OPERATION CAR WASH

Brazil's Institutionalized Crime and The Inside Story of the Biggest Corruption Scandal in History

Jorge Pontes and Márcio Anselmo

BLOOMSBURY ACADEMIC
LONDON • NEW YORK • OXFORD • NEW DELHI • SYDNEY

BLOOMSBURY ACADEMIC
Bloomsbury Publishing Plc
50 Bedford Square, London, WC1B 3DP, UK
1385 Broadway, New York, NY 10018, USA
29 Earlsfort Terrace, Dublin 2, Ireland

BLOOMSBURY, BLOOMSBURY ACADEMIC and the Diana logo are trademarks of
Bloomsbury Publishing Plc

First published in Great Britain 2022

Translated by Mr. Anthony Doyle

For legal purposes the Acknowledgments on pp. 179–182 constitute an extension of
this copyright page.

Cover design by Adriana Brioso
Cover images: [top] © venusangel/Adobe Stock; [bottom] © The History Collection/
Alamy Stock Photo

A catalogue record for this book is available from the British Library.

Library of Congress Cataloging-in-Publication Data
Names: Anselmo, Márcio, author. | Pontes, Jorge, author.
Title: Operation Car Wash : Brazil's institutionalized crime, and the inside story of the
biggest corruption scandal in history / Márcio Anselmo and Jorge Pontes.
Description: London; New York : Bloomsbury Academic, 2022. | Includes index.
Identifiers: LCCN 2021045824 (print) | LCCN 2021045825 (ebook) | ISBN 9781350265615
(hardback) | ISBN 9781350265622 (epub) | ISBN 9781350265639 (pdf) |
ISBN 9781350265646
Subjects: LCSH: Operação Lava Jato, 2014-2021. | Petróleo Brasileiro, S.A.--Corrupt
practices. | Corruption--Brazil. | Political corruption--Brazil. | Money laundering--Brazil.
| Criminal investigation--Brazil.
Classification: LCC JL2429.C6 A57 2022 (print) | LCC JL2429.C6 (ebook) |
DDC 364.1/3230981--dc23/eng/20211020

LC record available at https://lccn.loc.gov/2021045824
LC ebook record available at https://lccn.loc.gov/2021045825

ISBN: HB: 978-1-3502-6561-5
ePDF: 978-1-3502-6563-9
eBook: 978-1-3502-6562-2

Typeset by Deanta Global Publishing Services, Chennai, India
Printed and bound in Great Britain

To find out more about our authors and books visit www.bloomsbury.com and sign up for
our newsletters.

This book is dedicated to Lilibeth (Jorge Pontes)
and Lilian (in memoriam) (Márcio Anselmo)

CONTENTS

FOREWORD

Robert I. Rotberg

Most analyses of corruption, especially criminalized corruption, are outside jobs. Only occasionally are we rewarded by a consummately revelatory inside job. Fortunately, this book is a compelling inside job written by two longtime stalwarts of Brazil's Federal Police command. Jorge Pontes and Márcio Anselmo present a blow-by-blow account of the pursuit of the perpetrators of the Lava Jato (Car Wash) grand corruption conspiracy that ensnared presidents of the republic, parliamentarians, as well as the heads and secondary personnel of the nation's largest construction companies, its state-owned petroleum corporation, and a bevy of others.

The authors reveal in some detail how critical cases were investigated, suspects turned, plea bargains made, and detentions perfected. The book is full of inside information about telephone and wiretapping, surveillance methods (and mistakes), and of evidence lost and suspects who got away, thanks to tip-offs from politically ingratiating superiors. On the basis of specific conclusions drawn from material presented within this book, the twelve-year prison sentence for popular former president Luiz Inácio Lula da Silva should not have been overturned—presumably for political reasons—by Brazil's Supreme Court in 2021, allowing Lula to contest again for the national presidency in 2022. The authors, both ranking police chiefs with extensive knowledge of the many (at least thirty-two) phases of the Lava Jato case, provide strong arguments that Lula and President Dilma Rousseff were fully aware of a range of corrupt governmental involvements (above and beyond Lava Jato) and were thoroughly implicated in the knowledge of grand corruption. From the Federal Police optic, as presented in this book, there is little question that kleptocratic grand corruption, and state capture by criminal conspirators, was a constant of governmental procedure at least from the time of President José Sarney in the 1980s.

Lava Jato, and its exposure by the Federal Police and its successful prosecution in a series of exemplary cases tried in the federal court in Parana State, proved an opportunity to end the political impunity that had long crippled attempts to curtail corruption and strengthen honest dealings throughout South America's largest country. *Operation Car Wash*'s authors have much to say about how impunity has long protected their country's criminal political operatives from disclosure, arrest, and punishment, and how the successes in that regard, advanced by the temporarily exemplary outcome of the Lava Jato cases, have now been undone by Lula's release. Overturning his imprisonment means that criminal business in the Brazilian state has again regressed to the mean—to the detriment of probity and the rights of all Brazilians (not just the privileged elite) fully to enjoy human rights and sustainable economic rewards.

Pontes and Anselmo are critical of many of the ways in which the Federal Police itself has been compromised politically. Several chapters are devoted to recommending methods by which the Federal Police could be insulated from political interference and manipulation, and provided with resources sufficient to take on the problems and threats of grand corruption more effectively. They suggest better budgetary and sector priority allocations, and the decriminalization of many small-scale narcotics dealings. Pontes was a pioneer in investigating environmental crimes, of which Brazil has an abundance. Both authors advocate expanding and streamlining the operations and jurisdictional responsibilities of the Federal Police in Brazil (as compared to the Civil Police and several specialized police forces) so as to transform the Federal Police into an organ of the state more closely resembling the US Federal Bureau of Investigation.

The authors characterize a central feature of Brazil's economic and political life as institutionalized crime. It delays development. Perniciously, "no mafia can compare with a criminal organization that occupies the nation's institutions and wields the power to create taxes, draft budgets, appoint authorities, and approve laws." Within parliament, democracy is damaged repeatedly by the ability of those who work for the criminalized state to pass laws and deliver speeches extolling their results. "Not only do our legislators produce laws in the service of shady interests," they say, but they also neglect to refine the national legal framework. Legislative fraud is rife. And so the nation suffers and deteriorates. Graft is the star by which the nation's course is set. Major kickback possibilities overshadow real developmental needs, deepening the economic inequality of which Brazil is a global champion. Overpricing and price-padding are the norm. Procurement fraud is rife. Taxpayers are cheated endlessly.

Trust in government is essential to democracy. Tragically, Brazil now embodies the obverse, with its citizens—especially in the aftermath of the Covid-19 pandemic—endlessly believing that their government is up to no good. As the authors say, "The endless succession of scandals, absurd delay[s] in any penal process coming to completion, and [a] general sense of impunity form a vicious circle that leads to an overbearing feeling of impotence."

This book is a powerful indictment of Brazil's version of state capture. As it demonstrates from start to finish, criminal pursuits with corrupt goals pervade the very workings of the Brazilian state, but this is far from unique in the world; the same could be said of President Jacob Zuma's South Africa, President Vladimir Putin's Russia, Prime Minister Najib Razak's Malaysia, and (nearly) President Donald Trump's United States. The original Portuguese version of this book was published before the ascendance of the Bolsonaro regime in Brazil, but little has improved since.

As suggested in the book's conclusion, there are several ways that Brazil might resist further state capture and begin to reform its political and economic infrastructure. But unless those lessons, and the lessons of Operation Car Wash, are learned well, Brazil will continue to fail in taking its rightful place as an accomplished leader of the Global South, while its people will be the ones to suffer the consequences.

Even more than a powerful critique of the worrisome Brazilian political morass and its perpetuated corruption, this book is a powerful illumination of how good governments go bad and what can and should be done to save nations in parlous situations across the globe. Anticorruption crusaders everywhere will learn mightily from it.

Robert I. Rotberg, 2021*

---

*Professor Robert I. Rotberg is President Emeritus of the World Peace Foundation and Founding Director of the Harvard Kennedy School's Program on Intrastate Conflict. He was the first Distinguished Fulbright Professor of International Relations at the University of São Paulo. His books include *Anticorruption* (2020) and *The Corruption Cure* (2017) and is also editor of *Corruption in Latin America: How Politicians and Corporations Steal from Citizens* (2019).

Disclaimer

The facts and analysis present at this book are sustained in open access documents. In the case of names mentioned, quoted or referenced who are accused, the presumption of innocence, in observance of individual rights are always preserved. The judicial truth is the jurisdiction of the courts, which by law will decide whether the defendants are innocent or guilty. The opinions expressed are those of the authors and do not reflect official opinions or policies.

A NOTE ON THE TEXT

The Portuguese word *delegado*—the Federal Police rank of the authors—signifies a role in the Brazilian police and judiciary which has no direct equivalent in Anglophone world, encompassing as it does the aspects of all of the roles that we know variously as *investigator, detective, commissar, prosecutor* or *chief*. With the caveat that none of these sufficiently captures the nuance of the Brazilian *delegado*'s position, for the purposes of clarity the translator has settled on "Police Chief".

Chapter 1

THE ARREST OF MARCELO ODEBRECHT

What do they think they're doing? What sort of country is this?
Renato Duque, former director of services at Petrobras, in
conversation with his lawyer after being arrested by Operation Car
Wash in November 2014

Márcio Anselmo: We'd been executing a search warrant at the office
of Marcelo Odebrecht for some hours already when Agent Prado, a
colleague at the Federal Police (FP) who'd been working with me since
the start of Operation Car Wash, called my attention to a document he'd
come across.
"Boss!"
I didn't get the chance to answer.
"Yes?" said the businessman.

It might not seem like much, just a momentary mix-up, but, for me,
it clearly showed just how accustomed Marcelo Odebrecht was to the
subservience of others. He continued to behave arrogantly even in jail,
as if still surrounded by staff.

The arrest of the owner of Odebrecht, the largest construction
company in the country, on June 19, 2015, was a milestone in the
history of Operation Car Wash, the police operation which had
begun the previous year and would become the most significant in
modern Brazilian history. Investigations into the involvement of major
construction-sector players in a scheme defrauding contracts with the
oil giant Petrobras were advancing steadily, but we still needed proof
implicating the largest of them all.

The situation created public distrust, and we began to suffer a
great deal of pressure to deliver, precisely because we had so far found
nothing concrete on Odebrecht. For this reason this phase of Operation
Car Wash was baptized *"Erga Omnes"*: asserting the law "for all."

Pressure aside, everything happened in its own good time and in pace
with the evidence we managed to obtain. Even with an arrest warrant for
Marcelo in hand, the preparations for its execution were far from simple.

We had his address, but we needed to know the exact location in order to spring the operation, and we couldn't identify which house was his without first entering the gated community he lived in. So, pretending to be a prospective buyer of one of the mansions, an undercover cop accompanied by a real-estate agent and driving a luxury car gained the access we badly needed. Through some apparently innocuous small talk he managed to ascertain which properties belonged to Odebrecht and various other wealthy families: "So-and-so lives in that house, and the so-and-so's in that one over there said the realtor, eager to land a juicy sale."

It was a really big day and like every major operation, the team was on tenterhooks. In the weeks leading up to the arrest, we took all the care in the world to prevent leaks. In order to avoid escape or some preemptive judicial action, we had to keep this absolutely under wraps right down to the last minute. Even within the team, only a handful of investigators knew that Marcelo Odebrecht's arrest was imminent.

Most of the agents found out who the target was only on the day of the operation, already outside the gated community. We went there in three squad cars, one of which was armored, in case we had to crash the gate, which we didn't. There were nine of us in all, but only Agent Prado and I knew exactly how things would go. In the armored vehicle were myself, Prado and the driver, another cop. At six o'clock that morning, we arrived and informed security that we were there to execute a warrant. We met with no resistance whatsoever. Minutes later we were knocking on the door of the "Prince," as Marcelo was known in the inner circles of the country's construction industry. The executive opened the door himself. After a year of Operation Car Wash, everyone knew who was who on our team, and Marcelo recognized me immediately. We went through all the usual motions: I showed him the search warrant and asked him to accompany me. My first impression of him was that he was a cold sort of guy. However unflustered he may have come across then, I think he was stunned all this was actually happening.

That morning, four other Odebrecht directors were arrested too: Márcio Faria da Silva, Rogério Araújo, Cesar Rocha, and Alexandrino de Salles Ramos de Alencar.

Our first step was to confiscate all the cellphones on the property, and Marcelo's contained the hard core of his entire life. Later, during the analysis of the documents and objects apprehended during the search, we discovered that his cellphone was encrypted all the way through. It took us ages to decipher it and unblock the content. There were times it took two weeks to decode just five lines. One of our agents, Gabriel, spent over a year working to crack these codes. Marcelo created encryptions for absolutely everything on his phone, from company strategies to corrupt governmental institutions, down to reminders to spend time with his daughters.

At around eight, Marcelo's lawyer arrived, Dora Cavalcanti, and she was already apprised about the arrest warrant issued against her client. His lawyers had a minutely crafted contingency plan in place. When the teams started their raids early in the morning, a member of the company's legal team rang around to "possible targets" to check if "everything was okay." One thing that really struck me was that Marcelo's wife asked me if his imprisonment would be the five-day job or "the real deal." By that stage, everyone knew the difference between a jail term and preventive detention. Despite the apparent surprise, they were, in a sense, prepared for that eventuality.

That was one of the longest, most tiring days of the whole operation. After hours at Marcelo Odebrecht's home, we took him to the Federal Police Superintendency in São Paulo and from there to Curitiba. At around 11:30 a.m., Dora Cavalcanti arrived with hot lunches for Marcelo and the other executives.

On the way to the superintendency, Marcelo paid close attention to every detail. While waiting for the plane to Curitiba, his lawyers handed him Judge Sergio Moro's dispatch determining his imprisonment. Marcelo read it through and with a pen in hand underlined passages while complaining out loud about supposed errors and already drawing up a line of defense. However, like dozens of other such decisions, the determination was extremely well grounded in the investigation's discoveries. So much so that the preventive detentions of Marcelo Odebrecht and the other executives were upheld under appeal by other courts.

Once the arrest warrants had been executed, the teams proceeded to Odebrecht headquarters, on the banks of the Pinheiros River in São Paulo, in order to help with the searches that would continue throughout the day. The company occupies an impressive building, and I was amazed at the quality and functionality of the installations— something unthinkable in the "white elephants" built to house public organs and probably at far higher cost.

I arrived at Odebrecht around midday and the place was bedlam. A HQ had been set up for the operation in one of the meeting rooms and that was where all the seized material was kept. The company's twenty or so lawyers accompanied the search and tried to create as many obstacles as possible. It was a large team, including some illustrious names, such as Dora Cavalcanti and Augusto Botelho, successors of former justice Minister Márcio Thomaz Bastos. There were others too, who I didn't know.

Sparks flew between the police and Odebrecht's lawyers at times and for a very clear reason: "We're paid to cause problems, that's our job," the lawyers kept saying. Without doubt, the sensation I had was that Odebrecht had a far better structure in place than we did. The first team to arrive at the building consisted of roughly fifteen police officers, though these were joined later by other teams. At a certain point, we realized that Marcelo's laptop had disappeared from his office. We questioned the lawyers about this, and a laptop duly reappeared. The problem was, how could we be sure this was the executive's real computer?

The arrest of Marcelo Odebrecht and the other executives was a watershed moment for the operation in terms of successfully unveiling corruption schemes within the government.

Other arrests followed, and these would lay bare just how deep and promiscuous ran the company's relations with politicians and the occupants of key public posts.

The second symbolic moment was the arrest of the marketeers João Santana and Mônica Moura under Operation Acarajé[1] in February 2016. The pair were the most famous political marketing team in Brazil, the arch symbols of the limitless splurging fueled by the multimillion-dollar election campaigns financed by kickbacks on public works contracts with major construction companies. As staff and the marketeers themselves would admit over the course of the investigations, Odebrecht covered the astronomical costs of João Santana's services on ex-president Dilma Rousseff's victorious election campaign in 2010, when Operation Car Wash was already underway.

The third episode of note in unmasking and dismantling the criminal scheme at Odebrecht was another arrest made under Acarajé, albeit one that drew far less attention than that of Santana. Maria Lúcia Tavares was a secretary with decades of service at Odebrecht, and she became a key witness in outlining exactly how the company operated.

It was Filipe Pace, an inspector on the Car Wash team, who found his way to Tavares. Though one of the youngest members of the crew, he was a natural-born investigator with a bloodhound's nose for a lead. Incidentally, it had been Pace who'd traced a handwritten note found at the house of scheme operator Zwi Skornicki back to Mônica Moura. The discovery of this note, overlooked by absolutely everyone else, was the loose thread that led the FP to the gilded couple.

In order to zone in on Maria Lúcia Tavares, Pace combed through all the Odebrecht directors' electronic correspondence. On one file, tied to suspect payments, Pace located the initials of the user who had generated the document—luciat—and this enabled him to identify the former employee of what would become known as the "Bribery Department," Odebrecht's now-infamous Department of Structured Operations. A search warrant executed at Maria Lúcia's house by federal inspector Renata Rodrigues proved pivotal to Operation Acarajé. As soon as the agents found a trove of spreadsheets with code names and sums paid by Maria Lúcia, the team alerted us to a potential breakthrough. The spreadsheets were downloads from Odebrecht's in-house system Drousys, used for internal communication within the Bribery Department.

Maria Lúcia Tavares was placed under temporary detention—five days— but denied all wrongdoing. She rejected the allegation that the "acarajés" mentioned in the directors' e-mails referred to money and went so far as to claim that actual dumplings were packaged and sent around the country—an obvious insult to the investigators' intelligence. It was only after her detention was renewed that she decided to talk. Maria Lúcia was the first Odebrecht employee to opt for a plea bargain. Prior to her arrest, the company had denied all improbity and taken a conflictual approach to Operation Car Wash. Maria Lúcia's decision was made personally and was not discussed with company lawyers. By that stage, Marcelo Odebrecht had already been in custody for nearly a year.

Maria Lúcia's testimony confirmed that Odebrecht had indeed set up the Department of Structured Operations exclusively to process hidden payments to politicians and moneymen, but she had little of relevance to say concerning the origin of the funds or the recipients of the outlays. Nevertheless, her deposition was of immense value in slotting together important pieces in the jigsaw puzzle. One thing the Tavares spreadsheets confirmed without doubt was the existence of a nationwide cash-delivery scheme. For example, the secretary was able to describe in detail how money was sorted, packaged, and delivered to hundreds of politicians across dozens of cities.

This third episode was a death blow to the Odebrecht strategy. The information provided by Maria Lúcia Tavares soon led the FP to material evidence of a scheme that proved to be far more sophisticated than first imagined. The "Bribery Department" was structured just like a regular sector, with cash flow, director, organizational chart with lines of report, an in-house coded communication system, list of telephone extensions, and its very own database. A director would request a sum, another would sign off on it, and the department paid out.

Odebrecht was the perfect example of a criminal company with a parallel structure in place specifically to corrupt, flagrantly rationalizing and normalizing the venality with which politics is conducted and financed in Brazil. The secretary's decision to cooperate led to her dismissal and culminated in the fourth key point in the Odebrecht chapter of Operation Car Wash.

With the documents seized at Marcelo's house and the details provided by Maria Lúcia, Operation Xepa was rolled out one month to the day after Acarajé, on March 22, 2016. Warrants were issued for the arrest of thirteen people, including the executive Hilberto Mascarenhas Filho, chief of the "Bribery Department."

While it is true that the company's top-tier executives, including Marcelo Odebrecht himself, were all already in custody, Operation Xepa—phase 26 of Car Wash—was checkmate for the construction giant. Up until that point the company had stubbornly denied all wrongdoing and endeavored to disqualify our work in any way it could, through injunctions, attempts to influence judges and justices, and by waging a campaign in the press.

But on that day Odebrecht finally threw in the towel. The spreadsheets unearthed at Maria Lúcia Tavares' house were incontestable proof of its illicit practices. When she decided to say what she knew, they realized the game was up. That very day, March 22, Odebrecht issued a statement in the press. It read:

> After assessment and reflection on behalf of our shareholders and executives, Odebrecht has decided to collaborate with the investigations of Operation Car Wash. The company recognizes the need to improve its practices and has been in constant contact with the authorities with a view to cooperating fully with the investigations and with the leniency agreement sealed in December with the General Controllership of the Union. We hope the clarifications made under this collaboration contribute significantly to the pursuit of justice and the construction of a better Brazil.

For the first time, faced with a robust and consistent body of evidence, the company dropped its campaign of denial and began negotiating a leniency agreement with the federal prosecutors.

Despite the change of tack, an apology and confession would only be issued in December 2016, when the terms of the collaboration agreement—nicknamed the "end-of-the-world" plea bargain—had already been defined.

The plea-bargain and leniency agreement signed by some eighty Odebrecht executives was a bitter end to the tale. Since the very beginning, I had found the leniency awarded brutally disproportionate to the testimony the executives were offering. Worse still, the FP played no part in the negotiations, which were conducted entirely by the public prosecutor's office.

The plea bargains struck seeded an insuperable crisis between the public prosecutor's office and the Federal Police. Like myself, many other commissioners and inspectors working on Car Wash had been dead against these agreements. We knew the evidence we had in hand dispensed with the depositions of many of those involved. At that stage, Odebrecht and its executives had been the targets of four phases of Car Wash—*Final Judgement, Erga Omnes, Acarajé,* and *Xepa*—but the massive body of proof amassed was summarily ignored in sealing these plea bargains.

The public prosecutor's office showed no interest in the evidence we had obtained thus far and proceeded with its plea-bargain depositions, considered the ace up their sleeve by then attorney general Rodrigo Janot. Effectively, they ended up grossly overpaying for something they already had, as it were, in the bag. Despite having discovered the Department of Structured Operations, thanks to intrepid police work, the FP was prevented from participating in the negotiations—in the interests of "confidentiality," according to Janot.[2]

However, that failed to prevent one of the agreements leaking to the press before it could even be officially accepted. The so-called end-of-the-world plea bargain caused great brouhaha but did little to advance the investigations. Nearly two years since its signing, the deal has proved less than productive, while the executives are all back home.

Lamentable though this denouement was, it in no way diminishes the importance of the investigative work conducted inside a gigantic company, whose illicit practices have been an open secret for decades, albeit one hard to prove. For a long time, news of tender fraud and cartel formation in the civil construction sector was ten a penny, but the companies always managed to shield themselves from investigation.

Based on documents apprehended at the residence of a director with the company Norberto Odebrecht, the Congressional Investigation into the Budget of the Union began to unravel a parallel-power scheme conducted by major construction companies. A holding formed by twelve construction companies, and commanded by Odebrecht, ensured equitable distribution of public works contracts financed by the Budget. The tenders were defrauded or rigged in advance.

The report was published on December 2, 1993. The subheading read: "Congressional Investigation unveils corruption involving politicians and construction companies." Twenty-five years later, the news had changed little. The difference now, however, with Operation Car Wash is that the FP has managed to prove the existence of the corruption scheme and demonstrate how it worked.

Institutionalized Crime

Jorge Pontes and Márcio Anselmo: If Operation Car Wash's success in combatting corruption is unprecedented in Brazil, blowing the lid off the involvement of the country's largest construction company was even more remarkable, not only from the symbolic perspective but for other crucial factors as well, such as the sheer volume of evidence obtained; the way the investigation unfolded despite attempts to the contrary by the political establishment, the judiciary and big business; and the influence Odebrecht wielded in the rigged game of politics and the corporate cartels that controlled all the main investments made by the Brazilian government.

It was through this operation that the country really learned just what was going on behind the scenes. But, for those with decades of experience fighting white-collar crime, it was clear there was a lot more to this than just the dismantling of the largest corruption scheme in Brazilian history.

With different careers within the Federal Police, in terms of both years of service and the units we'd directed as commissioners, we'd never worked together on the same team. In the years leading up to Operation Car Wash, we'd exchanged some words on an internet discussion forum called "Diligências" (Diligences), along with Federal Police chiefs from all over Brazil. We agreed on one thing in those debates: the damage done to the FP by its long-standing prioritization of the war on drugs. The FP's obsession with taking down the drug trade had distracted it from its main function: to root out the corruption schemes that corrode the nation's institutions.

The discoveries made by the operation in Curitiba led us to a real diagnosis of the Brazilian reality: the existence of a new strain of criminal fauna, which we called institutionalized crime. Over the last few years, with each new discovery Operation Car Wash made, and with every new attempt to obstruct our investigations and prevent them from denuding the webs of corruption at ever higher echelons of the republic, we saw how the operation was coaxing out an organism that was far greater and more complex than the crimes under investigation.

When we look back over it all, we can see that, at different times, we'd brushed against what we now understand to be institutionalized crime. In the attempts by various chieftains to scupper our investigations, in the discovery of schemes that straddled different levels of government, this new breed of criminality had left unmistakable tracks.

However, even after a long time staring at the evidence, we still could not quite make out the morphology of this kind of crime, which was so massive we simply didn't have the necessary distance to see it in all its magnitude. In order to obtain just that panorama, we had to take a few steps back.

We only managed to garner an accurate perception of the phenomenon as different situations emerged over the course of our careers. It took us a long time to understand that the scheme, put together the way it was, had governments in its pockets and was boring its way into sectors of the state.

This system was like a huge whale that breaks the surface only every now and then, fleetingly, perhaps flashing a ridge of its enormous back, or the tip of a fin, or maybe just a jet from its blowhole. You could see something was disturbing the surface, but not its shape, full girth, or length. We only ever caught sight of parts at first, and splashes in the water, which is why it took us so long to piece together its true dimensions. In fact, we'd never even suspected this whale might exist.

For two federal policemen who had always endeavored to fight crime, there was no nightmare quite so terrifying as the thought that there might be a criminal organization embedded in the powers of the republic, way above all our heads, especially those of our bosses and even the minister of justice. It meant we were just puppets who would never be allowed to tread where the operators of institutionalized crime did not permit.

Cognizance of this mammoth corruption scheme gave us an overriding sense that nothing could guarantee the completion of our work and that all our efforts would be in vain. Comprehending this criminal modality has the power to inhibit and intimidate police and judges and, above all, knock all the wind out of their sails.

This awareness dawned on us at a certain juncture in our careers. As we began to have access to the upper rungs of power, we could finally see the face of institutionalized crime—and how it operated, how it distracts us away from it, how it intentionally sucks institutions dry, how it exercises influence and worms its tentacles into the highest levels of officialdom.

Over the years, we'd committed to memory all the situations in which we had glimpsed a sliver of the whale and by piecing together all those takes we were at last able to get an idea of what it looked like in full. All those fragments we'd collected over the years now started to make sense. Each experience, each hunch, was elucidated by the figure of that whale. Being able to denounce this phenomenon and show it to the whole world was one of the greatest moments of our careers. All the evidence was confirmed when a group of men and women managed to do what none had before: see this creature in its full immensity and drag the whole beast to the surface.

Operation Car Wash was responsible for revealing a hitherto unknown phenomenon. Institutionalized crime, of which we shall talk at length in this book, does not have the same modus operandi as traditional criminal organizations, because it does not operate outside of the law, but right inside it.

Together, we have over thirty years of FP experience under our belts, leading dozens of investigations and that was what enabled us to see that corruption was infesting the institutions we were supposed to be able to trust. And it's also what allowed us to understand that the fins and ridges that had broken the surface in isolation—the usurpation of the legislature by economic interests, the deterioration of the private sector, the attempts to obstruct the work of the police through the influence of the judiciary—were all parts of the same "leviathan." Often, in a bid to cover up the origin of their corruption, attempts were made to obstruct the FP, either by leaking strategic information or by stifling the investigations altogether.

This book aims not only to draw up a diagnostic of this criminal superstructure but also to show how, why, and by whom the fight against institutionalized criminality remains severely threatened. In addition, we want to help strengthen the work of those willing and able to tackle it head-on.

Toward that end, we shall tell our story, from our first steps with the Federal Police to the investigations we led as chief inspectors and which ran up against the battlements and ramparts of institutionalized crime.

Chapter 2

FROM NARCOTICS TO ENVIRONMENTAL CRIME

We have created a criminal justice system that is both perverse and selective, designed to imprison underprivileged kids in possession of a hundred grams of marijuana but not the politician who has misappropriated 10 million reais.

Luís Roberto Barroso, Supreme Court judge

Jorge Pontes: In August 1989, one of the two Boston whalers the Brazilian government had received from the US Coast Guard was zipping along the Negro River in the dead of night, buffeted by rain and wind. I was one of the twelve federal agents at the Amazonas Superintendency who had recently completed the maritime policing course and so was licensed to pilot just such a vessel.

The gift from the United States had cushioned seating, fiber-glass bodywork, with aerodynamic contours, and it was powered by twin Mercury 300 hp motors. Out there on the forest waterways, it was in a league of its own. Next to nothing could outrun it during a river chase—and they were quite common back in the day.

On that rainy night, none of the other graduates—all more experienced agents than I—were on hand, so the duty sergeant asked me to pilot the whaler on a stop-and-search operation.

We'd received a tip-off from our informants that a medium-sized fishing boat carrying a large haul of cocaine base paste would be heading toward a rendezvous in Manaus in the early hours of that morning. The cargo was apparently bound for Rio de Janeiro. It was music to our ears. Seizing drug hauls was an obsession at the FP during the 1980s, especially in the border states.

Visibility was low, the Negro was rough, churning with driftwood and flotsam, and the muggy heat kept steaming my glasses up, but despite my total lack of experience, the training we'd received filled me with confidence as I took the helm. I knew I was going to have to put all that theory into practice. Federal agents are usually chomping at the bit for just such a chance, but I really wasn't expecting to be put to the test so soon and under such adverse conditions.

The Boston Whaler was firing at top speed, weaving among floating logs that were visible only when we were right on top of them. A colleague was operating our single spotlight, but no matter how powerful the beam was, it couldn't be everywhere at once. While it was scanning the horizon for sign of the fishing boat, it wasn't lighting our path through the treacherous dark. But I was young, and the young always think themselves invincible.

We had a megaphone rigged to the boat which we used to order vessels to kill their engines so we could approach. The most experienced agent on board got to man the megaphone, making the rasping metallic voice of the FP resound on the river, barking orders that were invariably obeyed.

My comrades on that mission that night were all agents from the Operations Service, part of the Amazonas Regional Superintendency's respected narcotics unit. The DRE, as the Portuguese abbreviation goes, was known for being extremely active in the field, with agents who were highly focused and motivated, and who basically lived and breathed the war on drugs 24-7. At the time, the DRE was the apple of the FP's eye: a unit full of heroes, agents eager to chalk up stories to tell the grandkids someday. For feds back in the 1980s, that was what being in the FP was all about. We wholeheartedly believed drug dealers were the villains of villains, public enemy number one, to be spared no quarter.

The first two boats we waved down came up clean. They were practically empty and were carrying zero drugs. But I've never forgotten what happened with the third boat we stopped. It was a largish fishing boat, a one-decker, but roomy, and it had a huge hold, big enough for an average-sized man to stand up in without banging his head.

When we approached the boat, four colleagues jumped aboard and two of them went straight for the hold. The whole vessel was draped with this thick blue tarpaulin, covering what was obviously cargo. Having rafted the Boston Whaler level, I stood by and watched as one of the agents struggled to pull back the heavy canvas and reveal the load.

I don't recall the faces or the behavior of the boat's crew that night, but I do clearly remember when the agent trained the spotlight on the cargo. The air was heavy with expectation, because the tip-off we'd been given was that the cocaine haul was a big one, and there was a very good likelihood this was it. Our weapons were drawn, and we were just waiting to execute the arrests.

That's when I heard those words I will never forget:

It's nothing . . . just a bunch of turtles!

There must have been over sixty enormous freshwater turtles on deck, stacked one on top of the other and the same number again down in the hold. But our guys were so focused on taking a few dozen kilos of cocaine base paste off the market that they couldn't have been bothered with turtles. As I watched that vessel pull away, I kept wondering to myself how many of those reptiles were females, how many of those were pregnant, and what impact their removal would have on the ecosystem. I kept weighing the importance of what we'd found against what we'd been searching for. Were a few hundred turtles really less important than a few hundred kilos of cocaine paste or a hundred-odd videotapes smuggled out of the Free Trade Zone of Manaus?

It was the first but far from the only time in the almost thirty years that lay ahead of me on the force that I questioned the meaning of the FP's work as the repressive organ of the state. Right there, at that very moment, a suspicion began to fester that would crystalize into certainty down through the years. Whenever I saw the enormous waste of energy, manpower, and resources poured into narcotics ops targeting small-time drug dealers, it occurred to me that what we were doing might be not just a squandering of the potential of the nation's best prepared police force but an intentional misapplication of its investigative power, distracting it away from the true enemies of the people.

Put candidly, we, the FP, have our expertise and resources intentionally rerouted into activities designed to divert our attention from more pertinent missions which the criminal establishment that has harnessed the state does not want us to pursue. That cargo full of turtles I watched continue on its way because we were out there looking for coke and nothing else was just one of a whole deluge of crimes that slip on by unmolested while we're chasing the decoy elected by the war on drugs.

That night we went home empty-handed, but those turtles certainly made for some lavish dinners in the homes of the backward elite that commanded, and continues to command, the Amazon region.

My history with the FP had begun well before that night. Born into a middle-class family on the south side of Rio de Janeiro, my major interest was science. I enrolled in biology at the Federal University of Rio de Janeiro (UFRJ) but didn't complete the course. I decided to take a degree in law instead, and though I graduated from the State University of Rio de Janeiro (UERJ), I never actually practiced law and didn't sit the bar exam. In my fifth and final year of law, I sat the FP entrance exam and was approved. I joined the academy in 1987, and in February the following year was stationed at the Superintendency of the State of Amazonas.

The FP Academy (Academia Nacional de Polícia—ANP, one of the best in Latin America) ensures its cadets get a notion of nationhood, a good dose of patriotism, so that they want to go out there and protect Brazil. This is especially strong in the borderlands, which was my case.

The riskiest and scariest mission I had to take in my career was during my time in Amazonas, and it was directly related with the FP's obsession with intercepting drug hauls in the state. My supervisor at the time was one of the best federal agents I've ever worked for. João Gretzitz, born into a Lithuanian colony in the hinterlands of São Paulo, was a polyglot with contacts at the BKA—German Federal Police—and he had bucketloads of experience in major drugs busts. The plan was that I would go undercover on one of those three-deck Amazonian riverboats, aboard which, according to our informants, a group was smuggling a significant amount of cocaine paste. We didn't know who the smugglers were, so I would have a week aboard ship to positively ID them.

To look the part, I stopped shaving, and put on some Ray-Bans and a bandana, which was fashionable at the time. I was twenty-eight, but I looked a lot younger, and I had a strong Rio accent and *carioca* swagger. When I wanted, I could look nothing at all like a federal agent.

I got to chatting with the other passengers, and it didn't take me long to identify the smugglers. They were a group of three: a Colombian, nicknamed "The Chemist," who, I would soon learn, was responsible for cutting the cocaine, and two Brazilians, one of them a former member of the Brazilian Special Forces. I earned their trust, and with two or three days left to go before Manaus, I came up with a story to fish for more information about the scheme they had running. I offered my services as a mule to get the cocaine into Europe through Rio. I told them I had contacts over there and even showed them my passport. I'd been to Europe a couple of times and had the stamps to prove it. There were no smartphones or Google back then, so I wasn't concerned about them checking up on me.

Everything was planned and set, and then, during a conversation one evening, one of them pulled me up for talking too loud, in that typical Rio manner of mine. He said: "Watch yourself, the Federal Police infiltrate these boats now and then"—and he looked at me hard, point blank.—"But don't worry none, if there are any feds onboard, Sassá'll take care of it. With a knife. He knows how to gut a guy. He was a Green Beret, see . . . he's good with a blade. So you be careful now, anything less than maximum discretion is dangerous".

It sent shivers down my spine. I couldn't quite tell whether it was a genuine heads-up or a test. I managed to control my reaction and conceal my fear, but I sure didn't sleep well those last two nights aboard ship.

During the mission I carried a nylon carrier with a pistol and a HK submachine gun in the bottom. By day, I left it near my hammock (there are no beds on Amazon riverboats). My main concern was to keep the weapons concealed, so I hid the handgun and HK underneath a Canon camera and pair of lenses I had: a 300 millimeter telescopic lens big enough to cover them and a wide-angle Canon. I'd open and close the bag quickly, and all anyone would see was photographic equipment. Another trick I used was to carry my police badge inside my trainers.

When we were just outside Manaus, I saw some FP speedboats heading in our direction. So as not to blow my cover, the agents who raided the boat frisked me too. Just before it was my turn for a shakedown, the agents ordered the smugglers beside me to take off their shoes. I literally had to think on my feet, so I pulled off my trainer and held it up to my colleague at face-height, so he could see the badge inside. If it had fallen out onto the deck during the search, I'd have been made in the closing straight. I was selected as the first "suspect" to be questioned in the captain's cabin, turned impromptu interrogation room, where I identified the smugglers.

The mission was a success, and I earned a good deal of credibility right out of the stalls, especially among the more experienced feds in Manaus. It also helped me overcome the prejudice some of my colleagues had toward me, because I was from Rio and sometimes embodied the typical stereotype of the laid-back, work-shy rogue.

The two years I spent in Amazonas were key to my formation as a federal agent. Episodes like the one with the turtles, dangerous missions to repress drug trafficking, and the fact that I began to understand how the institution worked from the inside all marked me personally and professionally. I started to question our priorities and the missions we were asked to undertake. It was also the spark that set me down the path toward designing a specialist environmental crime unit, the Division for the Repression of Crimes Against the Environment and Historical Heritage (DMAPH), in place to this day.

Next Stop: The FBI

In 1990, at the beginning of the Fernando Collor administration, I was transferred to Rio de Janeiro. My new role was to provide security for the president's children, who lived in the city. In the early 1990s, Rio experienced (yet another) crime wave. Kidnappings were common, and the president's two heirs were prime targets. However, some moments of tension aside, it was a far smoother ride than my time in the Amazon.

When Collor was impeached, my mission was aborted, and the whole security detail protecting the former president's family was reassigned to Galeão Airport, considered a cushy number for federal agents. At Galeão, the workload was lighter (three days work, one day off), the routine was more varied, and you got to meet people from all over the world. On the day we were to report for duty, I got stuck in a massive tailback in Copacabana and arrived late. The inspector in charge of personnel was livid and sent me packing to the Federal Police holding cells in Rio, a post of far less prestige. Though it didn't seem so at the time, the change of assignment turned out to be a good thing for me, as I was able to study for the chief of police exam and also managed to complete my French course, which would prove essential to my career.

At that time, the FP superintendent in Rio, Commissioner Edson de Oliveira, was appointed head of Interpol Brazil by then director-general Romeu Tuma. Interpol was headquartered in Brasília, though there were units elsewhere too, including Rio. When Edson decided to transfer some of his headcount to the Rio branch, I was one of the agents he called on.

On one of my first missions, conducted jointly with the United States, we were sent to execute a search warrant at a hotel room in Ipanema, on Rio's south side, the temporary home to a Portuguese man suspected of various counts of fraud. We apprehended a mountain of documents there, including contracts with businesspeople and politicians from Brazil and abroad.

I was tasked with receiving a pair of FBI agents coming down to Rio to work the case. I analyzed the whole trove of material, sorted out everything that might have had some connection with American companies, all classified per language and country of origin. The Americans were so grateful they sent a letter of thanks to the FP. A short while later, I was recommended for the course in Quantico, Virginia, by Richard Ford, the FBI's legal attaché in Uruguay. I was up against another agent stationed in São Paulo, but as my English was better, I got the place. I spent much of 1994 at Quantico, home of the FBI Academy, nestled inside a Marine Corps training base. I availed of the opportunity to take a postgraduate course in criminal justice at the University of Virginia that was offered as part of the package.

This was the period that brought my formal training to a close. My perception of the need to structure the fight against environmental crime stemmed from my time stationed in the Amazon, and I acquired ample knowledge while studying for the police commissioner's exam, which I sat shortly before traveling to the United States, but it was in Quantico/Virginia that I really grounded my knowledge of criminal investigation and its importance, and the vital necessity of international cooperation in policing, something that would become a considerable part of my work from then on in.

When I returned from the United States, Edson de Oliveira was no longer head of Interpol here, and his substitute did not want me on his staff. I spent my last months as an agent working in security, mostly for foreign dignitaries. When the list of new police chiefs was published, I was providing security for the Queen of England's representative at President Fernando Henrique Cardoso's inauguration in Brasília. It was January 1, 1995. My name was on the list.

The first unit under my management as police chief was the Operational Service for Aerial and Maritime Border Control in Rio de Janeiro. I inherited some 300 open cases, most of them concerning passport-emissions fraud and crimes involving foreigners.

In 1996, assigned to the Internal Affairs Bureau of the Superintendency of Rio de Janeiro, I had my worst experience as a Federal Police chief. Internal Affairs is an infernal place, a real lose-lose game. If you don't produce the goods, you're incompetent. If you do, you're a traitor. Even if there is a sense of mission accomplished every time you take a bent cop out of circulation, it always leaves a bitter aftertaste.

However, I can safely say that if I had to choose between arresting a street criminal or a crooked cop, I would go for the cop every time, because corrupt police are far more damaging to society and they undermine the work of the police force in general. I was implacable in my role at Internal Affairs, but it's never nice investigating and punishing colleagues.

But necessity is the mother of invention. And it was there, at Internal Affairs, driven by the desire to move elsewhere, that I designed, formatted, and kickstarted the most important project of my thirty-year career at the FP: the creation of the Division for the Repression of Crimes Against the Environment and Historical Heritage.

Internal Resistance

In 1996, based on a diagnostic of the problems facing our environment and the way it is policed, I spent my nights and weekends devising a project to create a special environmental crimes division. My argument for such a division was based on the scale of wildlife trafficking worth millions of dollars, the FP's lax handling of these cases, and the growing importance of the area in general. I sent my proposal to FP headquarters in Brasília on January 15, 1997.

I battled for six long years to see my project make it off the drawing board, and once it did, I encountered obstacles that lent a whole new perspective to the power institutionalized crime wields in Brazil. The long delay in implementing the division was largely due to a lack of interest in the subject within the FP, which was usually content to serve IBAMA, the Brazilian Institute for the Environment and Renewable Natural Resources, usually in a supporting role.

Given the lack of response to my proposal among FP management, I decided to try another approach. I sent my proposal to Commissioner Washington Melo, then head of Interpol Brazil. He was very interested in the idea and invited me to set up an informal pilot program under the Interpol framework. I accepted the invitation. In Brazil, Interpol is a unit of the Federal Police, headquartered at the National Central Office in Brasília.

After a fortnight getting things up and running in Brasília, I took over as deputy chief at the Central Office, investigating environmental crimes as part of Interpol. In parallel, I continued promoting the idea of a standalone environmental crimes unit within the FP. After three years waiting (1998–2000), I decided to take further action. I rang Commissioner Wilson Damázio, then executive director, and asked to be transferred to the IRS Criminal Investigation Division, which handled the majority of environmental crimes. I spent the next three years positively "selling" and "promoting" my activities. I had to make a splash in the press if I was going to convince management to invest in repressing crimes against the environment.

I started publishing articles in the press and offering footage of each animal trafficking operation for TV coverage. I lost count of all the people who called me a "showboater" and "marketeer," and—to their amazement—I always answered in the affirmative: yes, I really did a lot of marketing and that's why I was on the verge of consolidating an activity that was important not only for the FP but for society.

Those weren't the only malicious comments aimed at me. Though I received support from a number of top-brass commissioners, including Wilson Damázio, Zulmar Pimentel, Alciomar Goersch, Paulo Ornellas, Valquíria Teixeira, and Paulo Lacerda, the older generations within the FP had a hard time understanding that environmental crime was really a police matter at all. This was, chiefly, a cultural barrier.

One day, as I was about to start a lecture at the FP, I saw one of the institution's "bigwigs" sitting in the front row turn to his colleague and say: "Here comes Pontes with his lizards and toads again! It's this sort of thing that is holding the Police back!"

It was interesting to note the expressions on the superintendents' faces as I spoke about sustainability, biodiversity, and the prices endangered species can command on the European market. I may as well have been giving a class on quantum physics.

This disdain for the environmental cause was not limited to the police. Before leaving Rio, while I was working at Galeão and preparing the first drafts of my proposal, I started keeping abreast of cases of animal trafficking at the airport. One of these concerned a German citizen called Marc Baumgarten, who was arrested while trying to smuggle 112 spiders aboard a plane to Europe. We notified the press and the story made a splash, largely due to a rather impressive photo of dozens of Goliath birdeaters crawling out of plastic containers. The next day, the economist Roberto Campos published a snide little article under the headline "The spider is ours"—a play on the nationalist slogan "The oil is ours"—criticizing the police chief behind the operation and the FP's handling of the case.[1]

Finally, on September 4, 2003, we got the green light to create twenty-seven specialist units exclusively devoted to tackling crimes against the environment and historical heritage—one per state of the federation. Though the DELEMAPHS only became operational during President Lula's first term of office, the whole control and coordination structure (DMAPH) was created during the second mandate of President Fernando Henrique Cardoso, in 2001 to be precise.

Not long after I assumed the post of DMAPH commissioner, I realized another facet of Brazilian institutionalized crime. Contrary to how it might seem—especially to my colleagues who endlessly scoffed at environmental crime—cracking down on deforestation and land-grabbing led all the way to some of Brazil's most powerful figures. We're talking people of influence at various levels of government and—why not?—the Federal Police itself.

This became clear to me when we were putting the finishing touches to the organizational structure in 2003. Almost ten years had passed between the date the creation of the DELEMAPHS was announced in the *Official Gazette* and the actual installation of the twenty-seven specialist police units. That's practically a decade of stalling and stonewalling.

Unfortunately, some regional superintendents didn't lift a finger to create their DELEMAPHS, and we soon realized they never would, given half a chance. DELEMAPH Belém, in the Amazonian state of Pará, for example, was supposed to have been one of the first up and running, because the state was and remains an environmental crime hot spot. Despite that, or because of it, the state's regional director of the Federal Police treated the implementation of DELEMAPH Belém with extreme lethargy, stalling for years on end. And he wasn't the only one.

Many superintendents, mainly from the North and Northeast of the country, were against the units and dithered on their creation. It was obvious to me that tackling environmental crime, unlike the "war on drugs," had no "distraction value." Quite the contrary, it didn't affect street urchins and small-time hoods, people on the fringes of power, but big-time businesspeople who had a lot to gain from ongoing and unhindered deforestation, pollution, land-grabbing, and bushfires.

Many of these businesspeople financed the election campaigns of local politicians and so wielded considerable power over state governments. There was, therefore, good reason for the regional directors' reluctance to set up the DELEMAPHS: they didn't want to hit the businesses that financed the campaigns of the politicians who appointed them to their posts. To avoid inconvenience all round, the best thing to do was drag their feet on DELEMAPH creation.

When they had no choice but to finally install the DELEMAPHS, they opted for Plan B: staff them with agents who had no vocation whatsoever for fighting this type of crime. Back at the beginning, I'd always thought that having few highly engaged people was entirely preferable to having a lot of people with no engagement at all. Interference from Brasília and state governments in FP structures has always been one of the main obstacles police commissioners and federal agents have to face.

But, in our case, the FP withstood often veiled pressures and frequently dissembled distractions, and, as an organ of the state, succeeded in overcoming these negative forces. Justice be done: there were many old-school commissioners in senior positions who stood their ground and defended the creation of the new division, despite the opposition, lack of political will, and regional boycotts.

At federal level, the minister of the environment during Lula's first mandate, Marina Silva, put herself at our disposal and always supported and demonstrated interest in the arrests we made of IBAMA functionaries, who are subordinate to her portfolio. Collaboration with the public prosecutors office was also indispensable. Over the years, I worked with countless public prosecutors dedicated to the environmental issue. Truth be told, I was never a soloist in this endeavor, and DEMAPH's success was due to the dedicated team of agents and registrars who accompanied me after I left Interpol.

The installation of DEMAPH coincided with the beginning of the inaugural phase of the FP's mega-operations. In 2006, a sequence of six actions against illegal loggers in the North identified a hundred or so civil servants involved in environmental corruption. Over the years, dozens of such operations—Pindorama, Feliz Ano Velho (Happy Old Year), Rosa dos Ventos (Weather Vane), Isaías (Isaiah), Dragão (Dragon), Curupira, Daniel, Novo Empate (New Tie), Oxóssi, Gnomo (Gnome), Judas Iscariotes, and Euterpe—in various regions of the country helped reduce Amazonian deforestation, a major victory of the 2010s.

By this stage, the Environmental Crime Division was up and running on its own two feet, and it was time for me to tend to my career again. In 2007, I was appointed FP Superintendent for Pernambuco (State of Pernambuco), one of the five largest in the country. The post gave me a whole new perspective on the Brazilian state and the power struggles that go on at state level.

My time as superintendent afforded some of the most edifying moments of my career. It was my debut into the world of police management. Though it was a hard period, it was one of great learning for me and showed me that sometimes we know strings are being pulled against us, but can't discern who's pulling them or even where those strings might lead. All we know is that someone somewhere doesn't want the arm of the law reaching into certain quarters.

When I took over the superintendency, I inherited a good team but one in need of a bit of a jolt. The chiefs were all excellent and the agents highly motivated and professional. My predecessor had prioritized maritime policing: issuing passports and managing the immigration posts at the International Airport of Guararapes. He had channeled little energy into major corruption schemes and executed no mega-operations, two of the FP's core activities.

I was intent on turning that around. I wanted to focus on taking down major local corruption schemes. I clearly remember the first team meeting I held. One of the police chiefs recalled something a former superintendent had said at his introductory meeting: "Don't bring me problems." That really resonated with me, because the role of the FP is to do exactly the opposite. We're here to cause trouble, to rock the boat. As my colleagues at the FBI used to say: big cases, big problems. Some of the police chiefs present at that meeting had been with the force far longer than I, but I was interested in the young guys, who seemed motivated by my arrival and that of Police Chief Rogério Galloro. Rogério was my right-hand man, a colleague and a friend, and he had accompanied me to Recife on this new undertaking. Years later, in 2018, he would become director- general of the FP.

Well, in my pep talk that day I made it crystal clear that I was there in Pernambuco precisely to cause problems, and the bigger, the better. I told them I wanted to hit the upper echelons of crime, doing damage where it would really be felt. Ground floor, first floor, second floor didn't interest me, I wanted the top floors, the penthouse. I reminded them that, in our country, the upper strata of the crime world are rarely rattled. They sure would be, some years later, by Operation Car Wash.

What I still hadn't realized is that there were certain floors the police weren't allowed to reach. When they started to get close, something always blocked their path. The residents of the penthouse had—and still have, to a large degree—the power to hire and fire our bosses and sign our transfer papers.

I had arrived in Pernambuco for a three-year stint as superintendent, but I barely made it half way through. Before my first year was out, Police Chief Bernardo Torres, one of the best men on my team, launched Operation Zebra, a benchmark of our administration and a chapter that will be told in detail further on. This operation dismantled a network engaged in contraband, tax evasion, money laundering, corruption, and crimes against the financial system, and it involved, we would soon discover, numerous agents from across the security apparatus. The investigation was a seismic event for the state government and led to my being "invited" to return to Brasília one month later.

I returned to Interpol and, in 2010, was designated the FP's attaché in Paris, where I stayed for the next three years. When I arrived back in Brazil, various colleagues were grousing about the government's dallying when it came to transfer requests. They were stuck in "the microwave," as they put it. In light of this news, and weary after long periods away from my kids, in Brasília, Pernambuco, and Paris, I decided to retire. I have been firmly based in Rio ever since.

On the night of March 17, 2014, I was watching the news on TV when I saw that Paulo Roberto Costa, ex-supply chain director at

Petrobras, had been taken in for questioning under phase one of an operation called Lava Jato (Car Wash). I immediately recalled a friend I'd played soccer with at the Naval Club on Rio's south side. His name was Otávio Cintra, an engineer trained at the Federal University of Rio de Janeiro. He'd been with Petrobras for three decades, with periods in Singapore, Santiago, and Houston. For months he'd been telling me about the frauds going on at the company. According to Cintra, a group had been formed inside Petrobras to "rob the place blind, across every area: bitumen, freight contracts, refineries, the acquisition of rotten stakes in dead oilfields, even the sale of the company's crown jewels." At the time, I'd told him that no one was going to open an investigation of that magnitude based on "rumors" alone and that he'd need to present hard evidence.

I confess I was even a bit embarrassed about not escalating his intel, but when I saw the news about this group at the FP in Curitiba, I called Otávio right up. When he answered the phone, he was just as euphoric as me or perhaps even more so.

I asked around to see who was in charge of the investigation. I called my friend Chief Roberto Troncon, who was in charge of the São Paulo Superintendency at the time. Troncon told me the investigation was under Police Chief Márcio Anselmo. I remember having exchanged messages with him on some FP forums online, so I e-mailed him about this friend of mine who had lots of information about Paulo Roberto Costa that he might find immensely useful.

Two weeks later, we met in Rio de Janeiro to hear what my friend from Petrobras had to say about what was going on under the table at Brazil's largest state-owned company. Much of what they managed to prove in the months and years that followed was prefaced that day: how the "lucrative" directorates were distributed among parties allied with the federal government; how the leaders of these parties then appointed directors and managers; how the cartel was formed by the country's largest construction companies; how the construction contracts were "padded"; and so on, so forth. This day-long crash course in the ins and outs of the scheme in place at Petrobras gave Márcio and Agent Prado, who was with him at the meeting, a mine of information about just what was going on at the company. Otávio even drew an organizational chart of all the appointees, directors, parties, and political leaders involved in the scam.

It's hard to say just how much agility Otávio Cintra's information gave the investigation. On that afternoon alone, Márcio obtained a postgraduate degree in corruption at Petrobras. And that meeting, conducted with a pleasant dose of casualness, ended up bringing us together.

Chapter 3

THE EMBRYO OF OPERATION CAR WASH

Everyone knew what was going on.

Alberto Youssef, money-mover
convicted under Operation Car Wash[1]

Márcio Anselmo: For a kid entering his teens, the news was far from good: my father, who worked in civil construction but had always loved the fields, was shutting the company down, selling everything, and moving out to the backlands. It was 1990, I was thirteen, my brother, seven, and we lived in Cambé, outer Londrina, the second-largest city in State of Paraná. In the streets and in the press, there was only one topic: the Collor government's eighteen-month freeze on all private assets.[2]

Our destination was Indianópolis, a deep-state backwater with a population of maybe 6,000. There was a village square, with the town hall and practically nothing else. There was no bank, and we didn't even have a telephone. News reached Indianópolis slow, as I'd find out some years on, when the newspaper carrying the list of university entrance postings arrived a day and a half late.

In the beginning, everything was new, but my brother and I gradually began to realize that moving out to bumpkinville had not been the best choice. Education and career-wise, it was a major disadvantage to us.

Indianópolis didn't have a secondary school, so when I finished primary there was only one continued-education option available to me: a technical course in accounting.

Though the humanities were my thing, I'd always been good at math and liked the subject. I worked well with numbers. Looking back now, the "coincidence" of there only being a bookkeeping course in Indianópolis proved decisive in terms of my future career, because it introduced me to the tools I would use to combat financial crime, corruption, and money laundering as a Federal Police agent.

When the time came to decide what to study at university, I opted for law, despite my father making it very clear he would have preferred agronomy. I spent two whole years playing catch-up, trying to plug the obvious gaps in my second-level education with books borrowed from my teachers and the school library. But it worked, and I made it into the State University of Londrina, which meant I would be moving in with my grandmother back in Cambé. Londrina was like a whole new city by then. I barely recognized the place. When we'd moved out to Indianópolis, Londrina's first shopping mall was still under construction, but after my adolescence in the bush, it was entirely different. It was there, in Londrina, at the age of twenty, that I set foot in a McDonald's for the first time.

But my father's aversion for the big city never waned, and he and my mother stayed on in Indianópolis for another twenty years, until age caught up with them, and it was no longer feasible for them to remain alone in a place where cellphones didn't work and there was no internet. In 2015, at the height of Lava Jato, I finally managed to convince them to move to a town closer to Londrina.

At the end of my freshman year in law, I was approved on the federal justice entrance exam and started supplementing my degree with some part-time work as a judicial technician. Like most students back then, when I reached my fifth and final year, I started looking out for civil-service exams requiring third-level degrees. In mid-2001, entrance exams were announced for the FP, one of the most competitive executive-level examinations at the time. The posts covered were technician, agent, registrar, and police chief. Myself and several colleagues decided to sit for them and again coincidence played its part: the chief's exam was on the same day as our graduation ball and naturally the ball took precedence.

So I sat the exams for agent and registrar and was approved after a whole battery of tests, including the grueling and dreaded fitness test, which consisted of running, long jump, fixed bars, and swimming. At the time, I went into the trial unsure I'd be able to get through the five exercises on the bars, which were eliminatory. Unlike the other areas of the civil service, police work requires a minimum level of physical fitness, so it's exercise or fail. My final year was madness. I'd wake up at 5:00 a.m. some days to train before going to work as an intern (the internship was also mandatory) until 11:30 a.m. After that I had my judicial technician job, which went until seven in the evening. Class started at seven too, *across town*, with the last lecture ending at eleven at night. It was a marathon, but it was worth it, because I was accepted into the National Police Academy.

I was initially approved for the registrar course, so myself and two classmates (and future colleagues) packed our gear into a Corsa 1.0, with no air-conditioning, and set off for Brasília, up on the Central Plain. It was a two-day drive, first to São José do Rio Preto in São Paulo and then on to Brasília. As we finally arrived at the academy, located near the satellite town of Sobradinho, we were greeted by a sign that I have never forgotten: "Your dream starts here."

My four months at the police academy coincided with the period leading up to the election of ex-president Lula, and I remember well the day myself and my colleagues went out into the streets to celebrate his victory. Back then there was no way I could have imagined that, only four years later, I'd be leading the corruption investigations against him. At the time, you could feel the hope in the air, the sense that the country was finally going to shed its old skin. And Lula's first cabinet certainly pointed in that direction, stocked with people like Cristovão Buarque as minister of education, Marina Silva in charge of the environment, and Gilberto Gil in culture.

At the same time, the FP was undergoing seismic change under Paulo Lacerda, then director-general. It was the start of the mega-operations, with the institution professionalizing and strengthening in bounds, and all with the full support of then minister of justice Márcio Thomaz Bastos.

From the "Trucker's Kit" to Financial Crime

My score on the registrar's course earned me a good selection of possible stations, so I opted for Guaíra, a town with a population of 29,000 at the time, near Iguaçu Falls, on the Paraguayan border. Not only was it a border town and major drug highway, it had the added bonus of being close to home. As is typical of all frontier precincts, the focus in Guaíra was drug seizures, and our bosses' obsession with producing press-friendly statistics reinforced this routine. Much of our daily work involved what we called the "Trucker's kit," which was basically a package deal consisting of stopping a narco truck, seizing the haul, and busting the driver for drug smuggling.

I ended up transferring to Guaíra along with a classmate of mine, Marcos, and we joined another agent of the same rank already stationed there. This new colleague had been eagerly awaiting our arrival, as his workload was Herculean. In fact, we were so snowed under we sometimes went a fortnight without a day off and hardly a night went by without our being called out for something or other. When I reported for duty at Guaíra, I was assigned to Police Chief Luciano Flores, with whom I would work again years later on Operation Car Wash.

Later, still in Guaíra, I was "loaned out" to the team working on the Banestado case (a corruption scandal involving the Paraná State Bank), not long before Operation Farol da Colina (Hilltop Lighthouse), which put sixty-three money launderer[3] behind bars. It was my first time working on a financial crimes case, and it was a real education for me. It was on Banestado that I met Erika Marena and, some time later, Igor Romário de Paula, colleagues on Operation Car Wash a decade later, among other agents who would play key roles in my career going forward.

Erika Marena arrived in São Paulo on a cold winter's morning. She'd been chosen by Paulo Falcão to lead what we called the mothership of the Banestado investigation. There, this hard-boiled chief of police began a career that would see her become one of the country's foremost authorities on financial crime, a walking encyclopedia on Brazilian financial malfeasance.

The Banestado case concerned a gigantic money-laundering scheme in which CC5 accounts (those belonging to nonresidents) were illicitly used to shift billions of dollars offshore in the late 1990s and early 2000s. Banestado was an avant-première of Car Wash, not only in terms of the federal agents involved but because of the public prosecutors too. Deltan Dallagnol, Orlando Martello, and Carlos Fernando dos Santos Lima all worked on Banestado operations under Judge Sergio Moro. Among those under investigation, the leading figure was another now-household name: Alberto Youssef, the money-mover who, a decade later, would leave the loose thread that allowed Operation Car Wash to unravel the largest corruption scheme the country has ever known.

While I was assisting on the CC5 Task Force, a new chief of police exam was announced. It was my chance to "get ahead," seeing as I'd decided not to take it the first time round. So I asked to be relieved from the mission and return to my station in Londrina so I could study up. What followed were months of intensive study and physical training, with one aggravating factor: there was now a cut-off time on the swimming trial—not something I found easy.

I spent the next months sleeping and waking among books and primers. Lunch was a time-saving home-packed sandwich so that I could study through breaktime. At the end of the day, I'd hit the gym, then go back to the books. Between court sessions on my registrar's job, I was able to read as much as I could of the Federal Supreme Court's dispatches.

I did well in the test and was approved on the course, so it was back to the National Police Academy in Brasília, this time to study for the rank of chief of the Federal Police.

My time working on the Banestado case reinforced my conviction that financial crime was where I wanted to devote my service and that was largely why I'd decided to take this new course. The content is pretty wide-ranging, with lectures covering all the areas of Federal Police activity, regardless of the sector you plan to specialize in. The key principles of the FP are really driven home, particularly ethics and teamwork. Some of the exams are done in groups, and the grade is key to your overall classification, which is what will ultimately determine where you get stationed. But while the academy encourages cooperation, it's also a highly competitive environment, with each future police chief eying those prize posts. Dropping points on a test could put a few hundred kilometers between you and your target city.

When Lula was first elected president, I was completing my first period at the Federal Police Academy in Brasília, but when the time came round for his reelection in 2006, I was back there on the chief of police course. It was, then, during an Independence Day parade the cadets participated in that I was in Lula's presence for the first time.

For those unfamiliar with it, the academy's military spirit can come as a shock, with all these straight-backed, cropped-haired, clean-shaven guys walking around in single line. They don't actually make us march, though there are some on the force who think they should. Today, the three to four-month courses follow a full boarding regime, which thankfully wasn't the case when I studied there.

During that second semester of 2006, Brasília was still reeling from the blowback caused by the *mensalão* congressional vote-buying scandal.[4] In its wake, a new tendency evolved which I'm glad to say seems irreversible now: a growing interest in financial crime among incoming agents. It's not an easy area. The work is painstaking and requires oceans of patience, as the investigations usually take a long time to complete. There are mountains of documents and endless paper trails, and we often find ourselves wrangling with hyper-complex systems, so the payback takes a long time in coming.

Historically, narcotics has always been the FP's poster boy and the recipient of the lion's share of its human and financial resources. Narcotics has the best equipment, biggest budget, and, for decades on end, the highest prestige. That said, today, one could argue that much of that has changed and that the corruption unit, while still second in terms of resources, can now rival narcotics for kudos and appeal. Seven of the regional superintendents in place in 2018 had come through the financial crime unit. That's a record number. And as superintendents get to decide where the resources go, this will ultimately reflect on the personnel, budget, and energy channeled into tackling each type of crime.

The repercussion of the major corruption cases we've seen in recent years and the growing recognition of the importance of this kind of work have definitely helped the area garner prestige. As someone who has worked at both fronts, I can safely say dismantling a corruption ring is way more gratifying, and generates a far stronger adrenaline buzz, than seizing 500 kilos of cannabis and busting hoods who'll be replaced the very next day. What's more, revealing a corruption scheme grafting public funds is incomparably more important to the nation as a whole.

The academy is fundamental, and it gives you all the basic notions and core principles, but it is in practice, alongside more experienced colleagues, that you really learn how to be an agent. Of course, in addition to that, you've got to have some knowledge of the financial market and accountancy in order to understand the accounting structures you'll come up against, and following the money is an endless learning curve. You need a bloodhound's nose and limitless patience.

Though my grade gave me a good number of places to choose from in starting this new phase in my career, I decided to stay where I was, in Brasília. On Erika Marena's recommendation, Police Chief Luís Flávio Zampronha, head of the Financial Crime Division (DFIN), in charge of the main *mensalão* investigation, invited me to join his team in the capital. So, on January 1, 2007, years after my first road trip there in my old Corsa, I drove to Brasília again, this time to begin my career as a chief of the Federal Police.

The Faktor "Faculty"

Working in Brasília is unlike working anywhere else. It's a bubble that moves to a rhythm all its own. The Federal Police HQ is less than a kilometer away from the Ministerial Esplanade and so very near the Congress building, Presidential Palace, and Supreme Court. If you go out to a restaurant, you're sure to bump into a senator, a minister, or someone of that stature. Like it or not, politics is in the air in Brasília, there's no escaping it, so you end up following events at very close quarters.

As soon as I was sworn in, I started collaborating on some pending aspects of ongoing investigations and gradually began taking over entire cases. One of these was particularly important and crowned my time at DFIN, as it was my first real brush with institutionalized crime in Brazil.

Operation Faktor taught me lessons that would prove invaluable during Operation Car Wash, delivering a "practical" crash course in how the system protects itself in Brazil. It showed me just how fiercely powerful political clans wield their influence over the judicial, legislative and executive branches, the banking system, and anywhere else they choose to cast their shadows.

In 2007, my first year in Brasília, the head of the Organized Crime Unit, Police Chief Getúlio Bezerra, my superior, sent me a report from COAF, the Council for Financial Activities Control, Brazil's financial intelligence organ, tracking some anomalous behavior— cash withdrawals exceeding two million reais—in accounts linked to Fernando Sarney, son of former president José Sarney. Made on the eve of the gubernatorial elections of 2006, these withdrawals were a possible indication of irregular campaign financing.

It was an important case, and there was no underestimating the power still brandished by this accidental president of the republic,[5] the undisputed ruler of Maranhão for as long as anyone could remember. There was no *underestimating* it, but I was still taken aback by just how deep it ran. Over the course of the investigation we had managed to detect and prove fraud in various contracts celebrated by the Ministry of Mines and Energy, long controlled by Sarney's Maranhão branch of the PMDB. Despite our disclosures, the ministry remained in their hands long afterwards—ministers Silas Rondeau (2005–7) and Edison Lobão (2008–15) were Sarney's picks for the post.

We also managed to prove the Maranhão chapter of PMDB was behind the graft schemes at the energy companies Eletrobras (the electricity corporation) and Eletronuclear (the nuclear energy company), and at Valec Inc., controlled by the Transport Ministry and responsible for operating the North-South railway. To this day, Valec remains embroiled in numerous improbity investigations.[6]

Even back then, Petrobras kept turning up as another sector under the group's "domain." As our investigations progressed we were shown time and again just how tough it is to challenge such powerful rackets. It was the most important case in my career at the time, and the result revealed to me that Brazil's institutions still needed to mature an awful lot before we would be able to dream of taking them down. Perhaps "mature" is not the right word. "Decontaminate" might be the truer term.

The first lesson I learned was that when investigating people that powerful you can never be too careful regarding leaks. One of the first steps we took was to secretly subpoena the bank records of all those involved, and our request was granted. However, we soon learned that someone high up the ladder at a regional bank (where the top jobs are de facto political appointments) tipped off the account holders.

This was a major blow to our case, as it meant the group knew it was under investigation and could now take all sorts of evasive measures. Something like that is unthinkable at a solid, image-conscious financial institution, but not at a small or public bank, where political interference is far more frequent and profound. It all comes down to the mob-style loyalty that accompanies a jobs-for-the-boys mentality. It was then, for the first time, that I really understood the chronic danger posed by jobs-for-favors cronyism at state companies.

In general terms, leaks are a constant concern on police investigations, and the problem is multiplied sevenfold when external information is involved. Internal information is controllable, as the FP is compartmentalized with just this in mind. But when it comes to third parties, the risk of leaks is far higher. This concern would reach unprecedented heights during Operation Car Wash, which followed a strict policy of the fewer who know, the better. To lock down sensitive information, each investigation was broken up into subgroups, so fewer people knew and even fewer knew very much.

But leaked information was not the only hurdle we had to overcome on Operation Faktor, not by a long shot, and, unfortunately, sometimes we only had ourselves to blame. During the investigation, we asked another FP unit to put a tail on one of Fernando Sarney's gofers, who was carrying a briefcase for delivery in São Paulo. The agents tailing him were instructed to follow him at a distance, keep a photo record of everything he did, and document his every move but not to approach him, under any circumstances. Unfortunately, that's exactly what they did and identifying themselves as federal agents to boot. They had blown our element of surprise for nothing. The gofer wasn't charged and the briefcase wasn't apprehended—even though its contents, judging by the frisson the event caused on our wiretappings, were certainly important.

On top of the leaked subpoena, the fiasco in São Paulo gave away our whole strategy, but we learned a lot from those mistakes and ensured they didn't happen again on Car Wash, years later. On all of Lava Jato's main diligences, having a tight-knit, cohesive team proved indispensable. Foreknowledge of arrests and raids was kept to the barest possible minimum. The fewer people who knew, the less chance the information would leak.

On Faktor, the constant patter of leaks continued until on August 20, 2008, just moments before the first major raids, everything came crashing down. We had requested arrest warrants for Fernando Sarney, his wife, Teresa Murad, and other persons of interest. We had search warrants for dozens of addresses in Brasília and Maranhão, including the TV station owned by the Sarney family. We had everything in place to finally make our move.

And then we discovered details of the imminent operation had leaked just days after we'd filed for the arrest warrants. Fernando Sarney, the main player, canceled a scheduled trip to Brasília and walled himself in at the family compound in Maranhão until a habeas corpus could be secured. At this stage, the patriarch José was Speaker of the Upper House, one of the most powerful positions in the republic.

We decided not to blow resources on executing the search warrants, as without the element of surprise, we were unlikely to find anything of use. It was a massive disappointment. First, because of the leak, and second, because the court overturned the warrants. I had worked so hard on this case it was incredibly frustrating to see that we kept running up against an invisible ceiling.

What turned out to be most surprising of all was that the string-pulling was only beginning on this particular case and included an act of censorship that remains unsurpassed to this day. The press had been doing investigative work of its own and *O Estado de S. Paulo* newspaper was on the verge of running an exposé about "secret acts" at the Senate. These "acts" were under-the-table decisions that were never made public, including the appointment of family members and friends to cushy posts. In 2009, the federal district court barred *O Estado* from publishing its reports on the scandal. It was an absurd injunction that remained in place until November 8, 2018—3,327 days later.

Once again it was made clear to us that the FP's investigative power had limits. The investigation soldiered on and culminated in various key figures being convicted of tax evasion, money laundering, and fraudulent misrepresentation, among other crimes. However, the body blow against Operation Faktor was still to come. In September 2011, the superior court (STJ) simply ruled our entire body of evidence inadmissible, throwing the whole investigation into the trash. For all those who had invested so much time and energy in those investigations, it was a terrible letdown, but it was also what the higher courts tended to do whenever we got too close to the anointed inner circle of politicos and businesspeople. The same had happened on Operation Castelo de Areia (Sandcastle), which had revealed a corruption scandal involving the nation's largest construction companies, and Satiagraha, a financial crime investigation barred in 2008.

The STJ decision to annul all our evidence was incomprehensible. Superior court judge Maria Thereza de Assis Moura recused herself, as did Og Fernandes. On the day of the ruling, Chief Justice Marco Aurélio Bellizze, from the Fifth Session, was called in to complete quorum on the Sixth. He joined Sebastião Reis, Jr., the rapporteur, and Vasco Della Giustina in delivering a unanimous vote to torpedo our evidence. Unusually, they reached this conclusion in a single court session.

The vote proffered by the rapporteur, Reis Júnior, was totally dubious. He'd inherited the case from Celso Limongi, who left the court in May 2011. In just six days, he'd somehow managed to study the entire case in depth and pen a vote running to over fifty pages. The main bone of contention was supposed to have been the admissibility of subpoenaing bank records on the basis of a COAF report, bearing in mind that the financial intelligence organ is part of the Ministry of Finance, but Reis ended up justifying his vote on the grounds that the wiretappings had been illegal and that the procedure should only be used as a last resort anyhow.

Their mistake was to think that we had based our wiretapping request on the COAF report alone, without other diligences to back it up, but we'd a whole year of investigation behind us by that stage and a wealth of material evidence to justify the move. The decision was simply inexplicable.

Unfortunately, we saw the powerful exercise their influence on many occasions during Faktor. Perhaps most pathetic of all was the fact that the person who had filed the annulment request in the first place was an employee at the Sarney family TV station in Maranhão. It was really tough watching all that hard work go down the drain through such brazen travesties of judicial process. With this dispiriting end to the investigation, I asked to be transferred to Curitiba and arrived back there in September 2010.

Nothing Would Be the Same Again

The year after my return to Curitiba, I came up against another obstacle in the arsenal of those eager to block investigations into major corruption schemes. Police Chief José Alberto Iegas had just been appointed Federal Police Superintendent for Paraná, and I clearly recall opening the *Gazeta do Povo* newspaper one morning and seeing his first interview in the new job. The title "We have to get back to tackling street-level crime" took all the wind out of my sails. I could not believe that the same small-mindedness I'd seen in Guaíra at the start of my career could still find its way into the top slots and in one of the nation's largest superintendencies.[7]

In the interview, Iegas said that his priority would be combatting drug dealing and other related offenses. It was a stomach-punch, because it was so out of step with everything the Paraná unit had been doing in recent years, patiently piecing together massive, sturdy financial crime cases against major targets. Since the Banestado case, the team had garnered an unprecedented level of expertise in the area and become a benchmark for the rest of Brazil. As I read that interview, I just kept thinking: "This is not going to work." Iegas was not going to move in any direction I believed in, and before long, just as we'd feared, the financial crime unit was scattered to the four winds.

Erika Marena went to work for the IRS police; Igor Romário took up the superintendency in Alagoas; and I was granted leave to do a PhD at the University of São Paulo, where I delved into international anti–money-laundering procedures. This "lull" in Paraná coincided with the period during which Sergio Moro was temporarily working as assistant judge to Rosa Weber at the Supreme Court. When he returned to Curitiba, Moro commented that he'd been away for two or three years, but to judge from the progress (or lack thereof) made on the state's financial crime investigations, it looked as though he'd just left yesterday.

And then, in April 2013, the situation changed again. Iegas left the superintendency and was replaced by Rosalvo Ferreira Franco, who remained in charge until retirement at the end of 2017. Rosalvo was an honest cop and a model leader. When he took over, he restructured the organized crime unit and invited Igor to come back and manage it. He also brought Erika back as head of the financial crimes unit. The team was reformed.

I came back too, on Igor's invitation, and among the "batch" of cases I was given was one connected to the former congressman José Janene, who died in 2010. Janene was one-time leader of the PP (Partido Progressisita) and one of the prominent figures nailed in the Mensalão scandal. Janene's operator was Carlos Habib Chater, the owner of the Torre gas station in Brasília. It was from this gas station that the "mensalão" money was sent out to be laundered at another company part-owned by Janene, in Londrina. In July 2013, we were authorized to wiretap Habib's phones, and the numbers turned out to be registered to the gas station. We could never have imagined that this would give us the loose end we needed to set in motion the operation that would change the history of the country—and, like no other before it, lay bare the entrails of institutionalized crime in Brazil.

Chapter 4

THE DIVERSION OF THE FEDERAL POLICE

The secret in every magic trick is to draw people's attention to something utterly unimportant, that is, distract them at just the right time, and that's what power does, power occupies your attention with all sorts of distractions so that when the really important stuff goes down, you're not looking.

Eduardo Moreira, former partner in Banco Pactual

Jorge Pontes and Márcio Anselmo: "In recent years, the country seems to have chosen to fight corruption instead of chasing crooks. That's the truth of it," said Carlos Marun, chief of staff to then president Michel Temer, during a meeting of the Brazilian Institutional and Governmental Relations Association—ABRIG.

Marun's quip can be interpreted as a thinly veiled attempt to get the FP off the tail of politicians suspected of corruption. After all, some of his former allies are among those currently incarcerated or under investigation for involvement in major graft schemes. His reasoning also betrays a distinction in his mind between practitioners of "corruption" and "crooks," one Brazilian society certainly does not share and the sheer absurdity of which has never been more apparent than in recent years.

His words are even more revealing if taken outside the context of his bungling attempt to reduce present levels of police investment in corruption cases. Marun is a recent arrival on the political scene. During his first term as congressman, he became known as a foot soldier loyal to the Speaker of the Lower House, Eduardo Cunha, before graduating to Temer's first team. In this speech, Marun betrayed his yearning for a return to the age-old trick of distracting the FP's focus away from our politicians' proclivity for venality and graft.

As said earlier, the illicit drug trade always served as a righteous diversion in this dynamic. The "war" on narcotics has enormous public appeal and for decades on end proved the perfect pretext for keeping FP attention at a safe distance from corruption networks. It has been, therefore, a gigantic waste of effort, time, and human and financial resources.

Elsewhere in his address, Marun doubled back to the same point, saying:

> The FP has withdrawn from our borders. It's plain to see that, today, it's the civil police and highway police who are intercepting and apprehending drugs. [. . .] I don't want to go into the merit of it: [. . .] this focus on corruption—necessary, certainly—did serve a function. But politics has changed, [. . .] and these operations have yielded their results. [. . .] But at the cost of exposing our flanks, territorially.

For the capos of institutionalized crime, there would be no Federal Police or public prosecutors office in the ideal republic. Of course, that can never happen, as they are institutions written into the Federal Constitution of 1988, and enjoy enormous respect and popularity today. So, if they can't abolish them, they can at least drain their capacity and undermine their ability to investigate corruption schemes.

To draw an analogy, what they want to do, and have always done, is fling a juicy steak to the guard dogs so they can move freely about the apparatus of the state and raid its coffers undisturbed. There are many ways they can get around the guard-dog problem. First and foremost, they can handpick a lapdog to lead the pack. It is always important to remember that the heads of the Federal Police and public prosecutor's office are chosen by the president. And, when it comes to the FP, there's a highly questionable relationship of hierarchy there.[1] Those in power tend to regard "their" police force as an organ of the government, and if the top brass share that mindset, if they believe they are actually beholden to the government that appointed them, then serious problems arise. This is something the public has to understand and keep a close eye on. The head of the Federal Police has to be very clear on the fact that he or she is in charge of an organ of the state, not of this or that government.

Another way of curbing the FP's enthusiasm is to "starve it to death," slashing the budgets for travel, fuel, and new entrance exams to replace retiring agents, for example. As chiefs of police, we went through countless situations in which our lifelines were squeezed under all sorts of pretexts. The prosecutory organs are among the most lucrative in the state, as their operating costs are largely offset by the resources they can reclaim. For example, the sum returned by former Petrobras manager Pedro Barusco alone, some US$100 million, would be enough to cover the salaries of 13,000 chiefs of Federal Police at the top of their wage bracket. If allowed to do its job to the full extent of its powers, the FP more than pays for itself.

The third way to lure the FP from the most inconvenient of its priorities is the main concern of this chapter: the war on drugs, the most common and reliable distraction of all. To extend the analogy, it's the juiciest, bloodiest steak with which to keep the guard dogs entertained.

The big guns of institutionalized crime in Brazil love the war on drugs and are immensely grateful for all the dogged effort we plow into this Sisyphean endeavor. And in this they have the public's support, as their antidrugs demagoguery continues to fall on welcoming ears, so engrained has the notion become that each drug haul converts into reduced violence in the nation's streets and homes. Unfortunately, that equation is not necessarily true. But it's a logic that plays neatly to the argument that the police are wasting time running after embezzlers and grafters at the top of the power pyramid while drug-fueled violence is spiraling out of control down below.

In addition to its demagoguery, this argument weakens the FP's effort and diminishes its resources, historically insufficient to demand in a nation where crime all too often seems to pay.

Skewing Priorities

Jorge Pontes: For the last four decades or so the FP has been "sidetracked" by drug crime, channeling time and resources into chasing weed dealers around the backlands of the Northeast, and cocaine smugglers across the North, Midwest, and Southwest, when it should be focused on the gargantuan frauds being committed against public funds. While we're out there playing hide-and-seek with small-time, readily replaceable hoods, we should be following capital trails, dismantling money-laundering schemes, and recovering the vast sums stolen from the taxpayer by corrupt politicians and top-brass civil servants.

For example, at various FP units, the wiretapping equipment is monopolized by investigations into the peddling of the bad pot. We've seen cases in which anticorruption operations couldn't get access to lawful interception equipment because it was all blocked up by agents investigating bulk sales of marijuana.

One of the most emblematic cases I can remember was during my superintendency in Pernambuco. When I took over the unit, it was executing very few arrest and search warrants, and my intention was to launch a series of large-scale operations to shake things up at the top of the state's criminal food chain and so reinvigorate my team, which had loads of untapped potential. To this end, I instructed my police chiefs to prospect possible lines of investigation that could hit the bigwigs where it hurts.

At one of our meetings, a small group of police chiefs presented me with some very promising investigations, but pursuing them threw up some bureaucratic obstacles that derived, fundamentally, from a question of skewed priorities. I was in my office with the head of pension-scheme fraud sitting across from me with a case file in her hand enumerating various fronts of attack. Beside her was the chief of Crimes against the Environment and Historical Heritage, with an important case involving the extraction and contraband of live corals by a gang supplying the international aquarium trade. Completing the meeting was Chief Inspector Barroso, head of narcotics.

As in any other investigation at the time, we needed to tap certain telephones, hence Barroso's presence at the meeting, as he was a sort of administrator of the wiretapping equipment, used almost exclusively on drug-related cases.

The other departments all depended on Barroso for access to lawful interception equipment. At the time, Recife had 600–800 channels feeding two receptors, Bedin and Wytron, but almost all of these were being used to tap marijuana dealers—a gross under-application of such costly technology.

At our meeting, the other department chiefs put forward their very cogent arguments as to why they should be granted access to these machines, but Barroso just sat there and frowned. I realized I would have to intervene in order to ensure equitable access. The narcotics chief remained intractable, counterarguing that the equipment was all in use and there simply weren't any channels available. He also claimed that most of the equipment had been bought with US Drug Enforcement Administration (DEA) funding specifically for narcotics-related investigations, and so he couldn't redirect their utility even if he wanted to.

The conversation was turning into a tug-of-war. As I'd only recently arrived and didn't want to come across as authoritarian, I knew I had to tread carefully in mediating the dispute. I wanted to reach a consensus rather than slap one department chief down in front of, and in favor of, the other heads. But the way Barroso was lording it over his colleagues, as if his department took precedence over the rest, I had no choice but to take a more assertive tone. It also proved a good opportunity for me to make clear, in a practical context, precisely what the focus of my superintendency would be—and what I believed should be the priority of the FP as a whole.

So I ordered the necessary channels to be vacated immediately for the environmental crime and corruption investigations. I then went to the regional judge responsible for authorizing most of the narcotics unit's interception warrants (international cases would require a federal judge), and she agreed to pull some of the less important ones, so we were finally able to free up channels for all the superintendency's units.

In conversation with colleagues, it became apparent that this was quite a common problem, with narcotics hogging resources at numerous other superintendencies. Unfortunately, it will take time and a change of mindset to redress this uneven distribution of human and material resources within the Federal Police.

Heavier Workload, Fewer Agents

As we've mentioned, misguided material priorities were not the only problem. At an institution as woefully understaffed as the FP, strategy is key. In March 2018, the São Paulo branch of the Union of Chiefs of the Federal Police filed for the release of figures showing the extent of this human-resources shortfall across the nation's police forces. The report compiled by the Personnel Management Department revealed a deficit of 628 chiefs of police, in other words, 628 chief of police posts that were vacant because academy entrance exams were not being held in a periodical manner and graduating cadets were not being sent into the ranks.

The month this report was published, there were just under 1,700 chiefs of police in active service, so the vacancies accounted for a little over a third of all posts for that rank. According to the G1 website and *Época* magazine, the same report listed 2,242 unfilled vacancies for federal agent, 917 for registrar, 107 for specialist technician, 116 for forensic police agent, and 387 for administrative agent.

Our staff numbers are the same today as they were ten or twelve years ago, though the workload is far greater. This is the main reason why agents need to focus on tackling crime where it will really make a difference.

It would be of enormous benefit to the population if we were to optimize our narcotics effort. The ideal situation would be to drop the "trucker-kit" approach in favor of what Getúlio Bezerra, one of the precursors in the fight against organized crime within the FP, called the "capitalist vision." A more clinical, targeted attack on the illicit drugs market would free up resources for the fight against corruption, embezzlement of public funds, money laundering, and environmental crime, protecting the collective interests of society.

It is highly likely that this "decoy" activity has been planned and cultivated over decades by those who want to see the real criminals slip by unnoticed while drug-world stooges take the fall. The "prohibition industry" is a lucrative one, and those who stand to gain the most from black-market practices are usually those who stand most vociferously against their legalization. One of the best recent examples of this was Carlinhos Cachoeira, a gambling racketeer from the midlands who fought long and hard against the legalization of gambling in Brazil.

Our prison population is the third-largest in the world, with 726,000 inmates as of June 2016 (National Department of Prisons).[2] Of this total, drug-related offenses account for the highest contingent of prisoners (28 percent). Almost half of our inmates (40 percent) have not yet been sentenced by the courts. A good number of those are people who were caught in possession of small quantities of cocaine or marijuana and so are awaiting trial in custody. This is proof if any were needed that Brazil jails a lot, but jails badly.

However, when it comes to prisoners incarcerated for corruption, the figures stand at a negligible 0.2 percent. Stepping up the drive against corruption would increase this number and so function as a deterrent, decreasing the general sense of impunity that surrounds this type of crime.

Putting more practitioners of corruption behind bars would also lead to the apprehension and recovery of vast sums of money and other assets that could finance drug-rehabilitation programs, not to mention construct, equip, and staff new hospitals. If we stop paying three times more than necessary to build each bridge or road and reduce the chronic burden of fraud on public tenders, there would be more than enough money to invest in social projects.

The war on drugs is a modern equivalent of the doomed Prohibition Act the United States experimented with between 1920 and 1933. All the collateral damage the drug trade causes today was seen back then, with clandestine distilleries, moonshiners, speakeasies, mobsters. Drug addiction is a problem that needs to be tackled through social policy, not militarized as a "war" that leaves a huge death toll and a whole generation of orphans.

Though it is one of the FP's constitutional duties to combat drug crime, it is more than clear that the way it is done today, it is an uphill battle with an indefensibly high number of civilian casualties.

When a business is driven underground, a whole gamut of "support" crimes is spawned. In relation to the illicit drug trade, we might mention arms dealing, the corruption of minors, homicides, robberies, money laundering, and the bribery of police, judges, and politicians. Drug dealing is also an "entry-level" crime and therefore a catalyst for other illegal practices. So until we introduce a national policy that takes a realistic approach to the subject, we'll go on flogging a very dead horse.

However, when it comes to the FP, we know that this is a cultural matter. When we joined—me in the late 1980s and Márcio in the 2000s—the corporation was obsessed with drugs. It was our reason for breathing, even more so in the borderlands. It didn't matter all that much whether you arrested anyone or not—the thing was to bump up the statistics, add to the tally of product seized. At the academy, all the cadets dreamed of was arresting drug dealers—and anyone who wanted anything else was a "wuss."

Even in relation to drug crime, there was a marked inefficiency in terms of planning and policy. There was no strategy for cutting off the drug mafias' financial lifelines. Investigations into money laundering deriving from the illicit drug trade were few and far between, largely because the focus was always on drug hauls. And given the difficulties of forensic accounting, the FP hardly ever followed the money trail.

Absurd as it sounds, the focus was ongoing after the mule, the truck driver, people who could be replaced the very next day. It was a strategy that was easy to exploit, as we could be induced to run after a fall guy packing small quantities while the real carrier took a whole other route. Brazil's borders are so massive, and the units deployed along them so understaffed, that it's simply impossible to police them effectively.

That said, the political side to the war on drugs is not the only guilty party in terms of skewing FP priorities. Sometimes, even worthy initiatives can end up distracting the force from its core objectives or hindering its capacity to achieve them. One such case was the Carbon Neutral Project, introduced by the Brazilian chapter of the Greenhouse Gas Protocol, an international initiative to curb greenhouse gas emissions. A partnership between the Ministry of the Environment and NGOs operating in the area of sustainable development, the Carbon Neutral Project was designed to map and help reduce the emission of gases known to cause global warming.

The program analyzed fuel and electrical energy consumption at public companies and organs participating in the project in order to calculate the amount of pollution generated by that institution and the number of trees that would need to be planted to offset its carbon emissions from the previous year. It was a very positive initiative that won awards as a benchmark in environmental best practices.

By decision of the director-general, the FP was the first public organ to sign up for the Carbon Neutral Project. Our forensic scientists were enlisted to measure the amount of carbon emitted, and our squad cars, boats, and planes took part in the field.

The problem in all this was that it fell to the DELEMAPHS, the twenty-seven environmental crime units, to plant the thousands upon thousands of saplings of native tree species required as an offset. The units' federal agents and police chiefs had to head out to the nation's primary schools, spades in hand, while the central command, DMAPH, was encumbered with overseeing the whole operation.

As it was an environmental project and the FP was showing an environmental conscience, everyone clapped their hands, but the statistics soon revealed a seriously damaging side effect to these good intentions: while our agents were out planting trees, nobody was fighting environmental crime. In other words, lumped with a task that was not in their remit, the DELEMAPHS were unable to do their job properly.

The Carbon Neutral Project put a sheen on the FP's image, certainly, but it was also a boon to the criminal organizations destroying our environment. In addition to neutralizing carbon emissions, it neutralized the FP's capacity to fight environmental crime.

It's a good example of how the FP tends to spread its resources too thin. By taking on yet another mission, its core functions ended up being compromised. Of course, when it comes to the crusade against the drug trade, the matter is far more serious, as the distraction it provides is doubly useful to institutionalized crime: internally, insofar as it sidetracks the FP and corners its resources; and externally, by offering the powers-that-be a handy and popular discourse.

It is important that we debate ways to change this situation going forward.

Chapter 5

FROM ORGANIZED TO INSTITUTIONALIZED CRIME

It doesn't matter how high up you are, the law is still above you.

Sergio Moro, minister for justice and former
federal judge at the thirteenth District Court in
Curitiba, paraphrasing Thomas Fuller

Jorge Pontes and Márcio Anselmo: In 1988, a United Nations conference in Vienna, Austria, released one of its most important international documents on the subject of crime, the Convention against Illicit Traffic in Narcotic Drugs and Psychotropic Substances. Known simply as the Vienna Convention, it was the organization's response to worldwide concern over the illicit drug trade and the vast amounts of money it generates and circulates.

On the occasion, in an attempt to stem the flow of drugs and drug money, the signatories to the convention took the step of criminalizing across their legal domains a practice that effectively allows the drug trade to breathe: money laundering. It was the first time that such a commitment was being made at such a level and with this kind of scope. Between November 25 and December 20 that year, a host of nations, Brazil included, gathered to discuss the issue. Only three years later, on June 26, 1991, then president of the republic Fernando Collor de Melo promulgated the convention, a decision quickly ratified by Congress.[1] In 2000, the UN published another document, The Convention against Transnational Organized Crime—the Palermo Convention, for short— which, expanding upon the deliberations made in 1988, tasked its signatories with combatting the practice of money laundering in their territories. The convention also carried a definition of "organized criminal group," in the following terms:

> "Organized criminal group" shall mean a structured group of three or more persons, existing for a period of time and acting in concert with the aim of committing one or more serious crimes or offenses established in accordance with this Convention, in order to obtain, directly or indirectly, a financial or other material benefit.[2]

Four years later, in 2004, Brazil ratified the convention, and the criminalization of money laundering—among other acts of financial improbity—passed into law by decree of then president Luiz Inácio Lula da Silva. The convention's logic was, once again, to attack criminal organizations where it really hurt: their assets. The classes on criminal organizations at the National Police Academy had long touted financial asphyxia as the best and surest way of tackling these criminal groups. One of the longest-standing lecturers on the topic was Police Chief Getúlio Bezerra, a member of the FP's old guard. In the 2000s, Bezerra was director of the organized crime unit.

In Brazil, Chief Getúlio was one of the first to argue that de-capitalizing criminal gangs was the most effective way of disrupting their operations, and he did a great deal to champion this view. Practically every class of cadets who joined the academy from 2000 on took his class, and he never tired of driving home the message: hit organized crime where it is most vulnerable—in the money. Bezerra's work rate and unusual profile made him something of a legend within the FP. He was cosmopolitan without ever losing his country-boy ways, and he was as casual in his mannerisms as he was in his choice of suits. He was a cop with a very wide repertoire and for that he was respected at the DEA, the public prosecutors' office, and among the federal magistrates. Once, during class, Getúlio was presenting his capitalist vision of policing and arguing that the force needed to target the richest, most powerful criminals, when a smart-aleck student quipped that there were only "hoods" on his beat. Getúlio shot back without a second's thought: "So—go after the guy with the biggest hood."

Although Brazil had already assumed its international commitment to fight organized crime, it was only in 2013, during the government of Dilma Rousseff, that the country finally devised a legal framework that was even remotely structured to attack these organizations. Up until then, investigations into these groups were hamstrung by the law passed under Fernando Henrique Cardoso, which was way too concise for such a complex strain of crime. As it didn't typify a number of conducts that are key to the modus operandi of organized criminal groups, it left too much room for contestation.

The months of June and July 2013 were turbulent, to say the least, with widespread street protests. Though a proposed minimal increase in bus fare was the straw that broke the camel's back, the unrest attained proportions comparable to the massive marches calling for direct presidential elections back in 1984. The June protests forced a "positive agenda" at Congress, with politicians eager to placate the people by passing bills that answered many of their demands. It was in this context that Brazil's current Organized Crime Law was passed, including provisions for plea-bargain testimony—an instrument that would prove indispensable in reaching the upper rungs of the nation's criminality.[3]

Regarding this law, it is interesting to recall the words attributed to then justice minister José Eduardo Cardozo by Ricardo Saud and Joesely Batista, executives at the J&F group, the holding that controlled the animal protein company JBS. In a recorded dialogue delivered to public prosecutors, Saud and Joesely recalled a revelation which Cardozo made to them during a loose-tongued chat.[4] The minister had apparently admitted to them that he and then president Dilma Rousseff felt they'd been tricked into passing this law, which, as they understood it, "was supposed to hit organized crime and the drug cartels." Dilma and Cardozo's intention was to pass a law that would step up the fight against criminal organizations involved in the drug trade, not organizations involved in defrauding public contracts. Back then it never even occurred to them that the law they were passing would come back to haunt them and be the very trap that ensnared much of their own government. In saying what he said, the former justice minister was clearly admitting the existence of a criminality that considered itself "above" organized crime and therefore—hitherto at least—beyond the reach of the legal and prosecutory apparatus available at the time. The minister's off-the-cuff remark is emblematic of the existence of institutionalized crime as an evolved stage of conventional organized criminality.

In fact, one could say organized crime has a clearly business-like structure. It has but one aim, profit, and it operates like a big company in pursuing it, with different departments, strategies, and action plans. As it operates outside the law, its hierarchy is well defined but occult. Members of these organizations only know the people directly connected to their particular activities—those just above or below them in the pecking order, so only a very few have access to the bosses.

There is another important company-like aspect to organized criminality. These organizations become multinationals of crime specializing in certain lines of business, which they adapt to the legal reality of the country in question, which might be laxer or more rigid. The criminal modalities are myriad: drug dealing, arms dealing, human trafficking, animal trafficking, black-market trading of everything from archaeological treasures to internal organs, and even money laundering as a core business in itself, that is, when an organization exists simply to launder the ill-gotten gains of other organizations.

In general, each group specializes in a given field, acquiring expertise and a reputation among its peers. This form of organization ensures the anonymity of the capo and so ordinarily shields him or her from investigation. The structure of organized crime is readily associated with the mafia or mob, in their sundry international incarnations, in New York, Japan, Russia, and Italy.

Analyzed from a historical perspective, as occurred not long ago in Italy, these organizations infiltrate sectors of the state in order to perpetuate their standing by laying down roots in the structures of political power.

The Official Platform

Institutionalized crime is a fraudulent system that operates with the blessing of the nation's power structures and support of a network that pervades all three powers of the state. If police investigations and judicial rulings ended up popularizing the term "Orcrim" (organized crime), now, in the interests of proper distinction, we must introduce a new abbreviation, "Incrim" (institutionalized crime).

Unlike the "conventional" criminal organization, institutionalized crime is not engaged in blatantly illegal activities, such as drug and arms dealing, human trafficking, prostitution, or racketeering. Rather, this type of crime is embedded in an official platform: the three powers (beginning with the executive), the civil service, the ministries and departments of the republic, its legislative and normative activities, in public companies, state-run companies, political parties, and the organs responsible for setting electoral norms, and all with a view to casing and embezzling public funds.

This kind of crime operates through graft, syphoning funds from public contracts for the provision of goods and services, public tenders, leases on real estate for state organs, and governmental disbursements, even to NGOs. It's infinitely more lucrative and less perilous than any conventional illegal activity.

While "traditional" organized crime thrives on the lethargy and omission of public figures, institutionalized crime requires structured, articulated action on the part of the groups that command a given sector, state-run company, or public organ.

However, criminally commanding a governmental sector, a large and lucrative state company, or a considerable public enterprise does not, in itself, set Incrim apart from Orcrim. Suffice it to recall what one-time Speaker of the Lower House, Severino Cavalcanti, from the Pernambucan branch of the PP, said to then minister of mines and energy Dilma Rousseff when insisting that she appoint an associate of his to the post of director of exploration and production at Petrobras: "What the President [Lula] promised me was that department that drills and finds oil. That's the one that I want."[5] No, the phenomenon we're describing here requires all three powers of the republic and only consolidates when their interference operates in favor of the criminal system, whether through legislation that facilitates its schemes (in the case of the legislature) or lenient rulings that benefit members who have fallen foul of the law (in the case of the judiciary).

We might try to define institutionalized delinquency as crimes committed by a group occupying *central* positions of power and directorial posts in state companies and the business sector. In structured fashion, these criminals avail of governmental and official frameworks under their control and their leverage with more than one of the three powers of the republic. While organized crime, no matter how sophisticated or powerful it may be, is always conducted in the shadows, institutionalized crime goes on at the very heart of power, deep within the official structures of government, and it is perpetrated by people invested with formal authority.

Where Orcrim's core activities are undeniably illegal, institutionalized crime corrupts and perverts ordinary practices and governmental activities, perhaps the hiring of a construction company to build a bridge to a refinery or a rolling contract for urban cleaning, for example.

When investigating common felonies, such as crimes of passion, we usually apply the maxim made famous by thrillers and detective stories: "*cherchez la femme*" (find the woman). In the case of conventional organized crime, it tends to be "*cherchez l'argent*" (follow the money). When it comes to institutionalized crime, especially in the first two years of our investigation, we had to adopt a whole new maxim altogether, "*cherchez le stylo*" (follow the pen). When dealing with this kind of crime, in addition to following the money trail, we've also got to track, study, and ultimately call to account the political authorities who sign off on the managerial or directorial appointments of those encumbered with defrauding and embezzling public funds.

The power to appoint cronies is a good example of the difference between Orcrim and Incrim. While organized crime co-opts top brass or, at a stretch, infiltrates a police unit, inspection bureau, border post, or airport control, institutionalized crime hand-picks and appoints dozens of authorities, all duly vetted and rubber-stamped, specially positioned to serve their criminal ends directly or to legislate and rule in such a manner as ensures their impunity.

When it comes to the *Diário Oficial* (the official journal in which all governmental decisions and appointments have to be published by law), the pen is the mightiest of all weapons. It is the power to appoint the minister who will oversee a major fraud scheme or to fire a director-general of the Federal Police who is not considered "sensitive and collaborative" enough to the needs of government projects. He who "wields the pen" can stock the Federal Auditor's body and the higher courts. It is by the pen that the executive influences the other powers, even to the point of handpicking the magistrates who will ultimately judge them and theirs.

Another important point is that institutionalized crime, with its armies of appointees in strategic posts and functions, has the power to draft and pass administrative norms and even laws that facilitate its own criminal ends. Where conventional criminal organizations use the explicit threat of violence to pressure their adversaries, institutionalized crime uses legislation to head off those who would present obstacles. Inordinate energy is spent devising bills of law that would inhibit or impede the work of investigators.[6] PLS-85, an act replacement bill, is a case in point. Currently at Congress, it would grossly distort the definition of abuse of power by police, prosecutors and judges, and hobble investigators with debilitating restraints. If the slew of new proposals were to pass into law, agents would have to give three working days' notice before issuing summonses or bringing someone in for questioning, investigations would have to be closed within a 24-month time limit, and investigators would no longer be able to strike plea-bargain deals with individuals already in custody.[7] These are just some examples of how Incrim tries to use the lawmakers' pen to shield itself from investigation and prosecution. Thankfully, none of these measures made it through Congress.

With Operation Car Wash, sectors of the Brazilian political elite feeling the net closing around them set the ball rolling on these bills with the obvious intention of intimidating prosecutors, judges, and Federal police officers. At no time did either house of the Brazilian legislature endeavor to foot motions that would have strengthened and protected law enforcement. Quite the contrary.

Furthermore, administrative vendettas, even more common than legislative grudges, saw investigators transferred or removed, chiefs replaced, staff cut, and budgets slashed at the agencies pursuing penal prosecutions.

By way of example, there was the recent closure of a state police agency that was investigating corruption schemes that implicated certain public authorities.[8] This was done despite the population's growing clamor against corruption.

The territoriality of criminal conduct is yet another difference between these two organizational models. Where organized crime maps out city blocks, staking its claim to everything between this bridge and that canal, delimiting the turf its foot soldiers can patrol, institutionalized crime shares out posts, state companies, ministries, and development secretaries, not to mention international sporting mega-events.

The Office of the President's Chief of Staff

It's hard to pinpoint when exactly crime became institutionalized in Brazil; it was really the culmination of the long-standing deterioration and gradual corruption of public administration. It is common knowledge that hands have always been in the national cookie jar, and that payola and graft are endemic to the national culture and behavior. The notion that public funds and property belong to no one rather than everyone is imbued with the sinister logic that they can be appropriated at will. Corruption is accepted as business as usual in corporate relations with the public sector. Palms are greased without a second thought.

In parallel with this culture of complacency toward practices of corruption, for decades now we have had a model of electoral funding that sees incumbent governors and congresspeople beholden to their under-the-table donors right from the start of their mandates. The main political parties and their leading lights have, historically, been elected on the back of campaigns bankrolled by major companies.

Ministries, secretariats, state directorates, and a whole plethora of lesser posts have become swag to be distributed as per backroom deals sealed during the electoral campaigns. A veritable mechanism of jobbery and fraud kicks in to favor the interests of generous corporate donors so as to keep the funding coming and the vicious circle rotating.

These schemes observe no ideological distinctions and operate just as well under governments left, right, and center. As Operation Car

Wash and earlier investigations have shown, and convictions have confirmed, the political parties in Brazil function as mafias.

Politics is the mainstay of institutionalized crime, because it provides the opportunity and access to the operators and jobbers. The chance to make money through fraud prevails over any party philosophy or ideology. To a certain degree, the allotment of sectors and services apes the modus operandi of mafia clans, who strengthen criminal activity overall by cutting up cities and regions into inviolable "turfs."

The "Mensalão" case, loosely translated as "monthly payoff," is illustrative of how a congressional majority can be secured through corruption. The police investigation into these monthly stipends which Lula's PT (Brazilian Workers' Party) government (2002–10) paid to congressmen from political parties across the political spectrum confirms the readiness of these organizations to fall in line with and consolidate institutionalized crime. We're not talking here about a subgroup, a political microcosm, or just one particular party, much less the newbies and fringe figures, but the top brass across all the major parties, from the lowest orders to the highest rungs. In his final report on the case, Police Chief Luís Flávio Zampronha,[9] who led the Mensalão investigation between 2005 and 2011, clearly explained that it was the party leaders or whips who received the bulk payments from Marcos Valério, the operator of the scheme, and disbursed it to the rank and file.

Supreme Court judge Joaquim Barbosa, rapporteur of the Mensalão case at the Supreme Court, echoed Zampronha's conclusion, saying: "The beneficiaries of the parties other than the Partido dos Trabalhadores were the House leaders or party presidents, who determined and enforced the party line at Congress."

In his closing report, Zampronha also broached the theme of the institutionalization of crime. While explaining how Marcos Valério's scheme was assembled, the chief said that in order to have a better overview of how it worked, we need to first analyze the political and economic dimensions involved. He concludes: "One might say that the political parties are, in a sense, at the mercy of particular interests, as economic leverage is frequently used to obtain political influence."

During the investigation spearheaded by Zampronha, the president of the republic, Luiz Inácio Lula da Silva, was called in for questioning, but the request was barred by then attorney general Antonio Fernando de Souza. A decade since the scandal, and after the revelation of countless others involving the PT, one can say that Antonio Fernando was ill-advised in his decision.

The degree of commitment shown by the party leaders, itself an indication that Brazil's elected officials are certainly no strangers to this kind of systemic corruption, can be measured by other means too. In December 2017, all of the major parties were presided over by people under investigation or facing serious accusations. With differing degrees of complexity, the leaders of PMDB, PSDB, PT, DEM, PP, PR, PRB, PSD, and Solidariedade were all implicated in some manner of malfeasance. Political heavyweights like Aécio Neves (PSDB), Romero Jucá (MDB), and Agripino Maia (DEM) occupied the presidency of their respective parties while under criminal investigation for involvement in corruption.

Though corruption had always been endemic in relations between the executive and the legislature, it all became more sophisticated during Lula's first term of office. In order to understand this leap in the institutionalization of corruption, we must first go back to the origins of the Mensalão. When it comes to the organization and functioning of a corruption scheme inside the apparatus of the state, one factor is crucial: the hands-on engagement of the president's chief of staff. Given the proximity of this post to the presidential cabinet, the authority it wields, its capacity to coordinate and control the ministries and other sectors of government, as well as to sign off on appointments to a gamut of cushy state jobs, the chief of staff's office can operate as a sort of holding for all the graft schemes ransacking the Treasury from all sides.

If corruption was wholesale in successive governments, "ground zero" of its institutionalization was when the position of chief of staff became its overseer within the public machine. The sequence of PT chiefs of staff indicted for or accused of corruption is no coincidence. The two most powerful, José Dirceu and Antonio Palocci, were both convicted and jailed. Erenice Guerra,[10] Gleisi Hoffmann,[11] Jaques Wagner,[12] and Aloizio Mercadante[13] are all under investigation or facing penal processes. Preserving the tradition after the impeachment of Dilma Rousseff, Eliseu Padilha,[14] from the MDB, was also brought before the Supreme Court.

José Dirceu is a classic case. After commanding the scheme to purchase the allegiance of other political parties during the presidential and gubernatorial campaigns, he was appointed Lula's chief of staff, where he then launched the congressional vote-buying scheme for which he was tried and convicted by the Supreme Court. In his concluding statement on November 12, 2012, rapporteur of the case Joaquim Barbosa described Dirceu's remit:

The accused held one of the most important functions in the Republic. He vitiated that function by taking key decisions that would ensure the success of a criminal undertaking [. . .] The body of evidence [. . .] places the then-Chief of Staff at the head of an organization that pledged illicit payments to members of congress in return for their assured support for the Government.

Dirceu was as pivotal a figure in the Petrolão scheme as he was in the Mensalão. In the so-called Petrolão, he put political cronies into key posts within state-owned oil giant Petrobras, the country's largest company, in order to grease the cogs of a mammoth corruption scheme.

It is worth recalling at this point that ex-president of the republic Dilma Rousseff (another former chief of staff), seeing the net close around her mentor Lula, tried to appoint him to precisely this post.

The centralization of corruption schemes under federal government command formed the kernel of the convictions of both José Dirceu (Mensalão) and Lula (Car Wash). If, in the former case, it was proved that Dirceu was the architect behind a congressional vote-buying scheme, in the latter, it was shown that Lula was repeatedly corrupted by major construction companies eager to obtain fat government contracts.

The institutionalization of corruption within the federal government during the PT years can be gauged from the high level of the posts those accused or convicted of graft occupied within it. In addition to the chiefs of staff mentioned earlier, one minister of finance was convicted and jailed (Antonio Palocci) and another charged (Guido Mantega), one minister of planning was charged and placed under preventive imprisonment (Paulo Bernardo), two PT Treasurers were convicted and jailed (Delúbio Soares and João Vaccari), two former PT presidents faced or are facing charges (José Genoino and Gleisi Hoffmann), another former president of the republic is under investigation (Dilma Rousseff), the house leader of Dilma's government, Senator Delcídio do Amaral, was arrested in the act of conspiring against Operation Car Wash, and a former director of Banco do Brasil (Henrique Pizzolato) and a president of Petrobras (Aldemir Bendine) were both handed jail sentences.

The Paradox of the FP under Lula

There is an apparent contradiction between the growth of institutionalized crime and the way the FP operated during the PT governments. On one hand, this morphology of crime reached its zenith with José Dirceu as chief of staff; on the other, the FP attained an unprecedented level of operational and institutional maturity during precisely the same period. This level of excellence and efficiency led to the string of mega-operations that began in 2003.

At the center of this was Márcio Thomaz Bastos, one of the most influential criminal lawyers in the country and justice minister during Lula's first term of office. With rare exceptions, justice ministers in recent mandates ended up becoming mere advisors to presidents embroiled in corruption investigations, and Thomaz Bastos was no different. In fact, he was the author of the nefarious defense used by those involved in the mensalão scandal to the effect that the vote-buying scheme Lula had in place, and which was proved beyond doubt by the investigations and witness testimony at the time, was about distributing not bribe money but off-the-books campaign funding. In other words, it was all just under-the-table campaign financing, a minor matter of electoral fraud (because the resources had not been declared to the electoral court) and not, perish the thought, *corruption.*[15]

Years later, back working as a lawyer and legal consultant, Thomaz Bastos was once again the main strategist behind the defense used by the cartel and politicians involved in the Petrobras scandal. His death, in 2014, with Car Wash reaching its height, severely rattled their front line of defense.

But Thomaz Bastos also deserves enormous credit for the vast improvement seen at the FP over the last fifteen years. When he was appointed minister of justice in 2003, his choice for director-general of the Federal Police was the retired chief Paulo Fernando da Costa Lacerda, who would go on to become one of the best occupants of the post in the history of the corporation. It was Paulo Lacerda who, with the help of executive director Zulmar Pimentel, transformed the FP into a veritable machine when it came to structuring and executing major investigations and operations. His tenure was a turning point in our capacity to target the upper echelons of corruption and fraud at public organs, leaving behind the war-on-drugs culture of previous general directorships.

Paulo Lacerda's administration relaunched entrance exams to fill vacant posts and obtained unrivaled expertise in planning and operational coordination, vital to the viability of actions involving hundreds of agents and multiple targets. It was also under Lacerda that the best and most effective use of the Guardião lawful interception system was made. Databases were created and tools developed for the analysis and organization of operational information. Some of these areas simply reached maturity during the "Paulo Lacerda era," but others were created from scratch. When all is said and done, the FP advanced in leaps and bounds under the general directorship of Paulo Lacerda, the man chosen and appointed by Thomaz Bastos.

On the eternal director-general of the FP's mega-op phase, I [Jorge Pontes] remember my participation in what was perhaps one of his last missions at the corporation. Lacerda was my immediate superior when I was superintendent in Pernambuco, but we weren't close. He was very serious and reserved, a walking example of how a Federal Police chief ought to behave. He avoided media exposure and was extremely discreet. My conversations with him at his meetings with superintendents were considered and rehearsed internally to avoid mishaps.

At the time, 2007, I was the newest of the twenty-seven regional FP superintendents and perhaps for that reason the least vocal. One day, soon after I arrived in Recife, I realized that we didn't have a unit in Fernando de Noronha. This archipelago (one main island and a string of islets and crags) sits in the Atlantic Ocean 545 kilometers from Recife and was the only piece of Brazil that didn't have a Federal Police presence. I invited the chiefs of the narcotics, environmental crime, and immigration units, and we set off on a three-day mission to the island in order to assess the need for an FP precinct there and to prospect potential sites.

I came back to Recife feeling really excited about the project. After two weeks of studies and meetings with the state authority, I rang Chief Paulo to discuss the post. Our conversation went so well that I managed to convince him to visit the island to see, in loco, how the work was going on in the far-Atlantic installation.

A few days later, Chief Paulo called me back and scheduled our visit. We flew out there in the company of Alciomar Goersch, his director of logistics, and we spent two very pleasant days in Noronha, as guests at the official residence of the island's administrator. On this occasion I was able to get to know a more relaxed version of Chief Paulo, a cosmopolitan wine-connoisseur who was interested in environmental preservation. And we had two things in common: a love of sunbathing and Rio's eternal Flamengo.

We surveilled the area by land and sea, and he confessed to me that it was one of the few moments in all his years at the head of the FP that he had actually been able to relax. This time in Noronha broke the ice for us. As a director-general, Chief Paulo was even-tempered and intellectually refined, a man of calm demeanor and pleasant speech. I could see how those days away had served as a sort of decompression stop for him, and when we parted, he said he would very much like to return for the inauguration of the post.

In Rio de Janeiro I invited Alexandre Saraiva, the best chief we had in the environmental area, and I tasked him with getting the Fernando de Noronha post up and running at top speed. A few days later, Brazil received the news that Paulo Lacerda was being replaced as director-general of the Federal Police.

Obviously he wasn't present at the inauguration in Noronha, and I almost wasn't either. In truth, it was my last act as regional superintendent and then only as a special concession on the part of the new director—after all, it was a project planned and executed by my administration. The next day, I returned to Recife to attend the swearing-in of my replacement as superintendent.

The FP was not the only protagonist in this process of transformation that led to Operation Car Wash and the most successful attempt to dismantle the oligarchies behind institutionalized crime. Criminal prosecution is a tripod, and, in the first years of the 2000s, the lower federal courts underwent a similar revival and renewal through an influx of fresh talent. At the same time, the public prosecutors' office, the third leg of the tripod, achieved an advanced level of maturity of its own. The same occurred with the Inland Revenue Service, an organ whose collaboration is vital to the success of operations involving money laundering.

It was also at this time that COAF, the Council for Financial Activities Control, Brazil's financial intelligence organ, was set up, with Antonio Gustavo Rodrigues as chief officer. Financial intelligence is another fundamental link in the chain, as it allows us to follow the money. COAF is notified of all potentially suspect financial operations in sectors considered vulnerable to money laundering, mostly connected to the financial markets. It then analyzes these operations and forwards them (if necessary) to law enforcement.

So, while Márcio Thomaz Bastos will go down in history as one of the main formulators of the defense strategies of major players implicated in institutionalized crime, we cannot ignore the decisive role he played in strengthening the Federal Police, an achievement which the PT governments made a real song and dance about in their electoral propaganda, with former president Lula leading the way. At the end of the day, the government that did the most to institutionalize crime in Brazil was also, and paradoxically, the government behind the transformation of the very institution that would eventually be the downfall of its most illustrious figures.

However, while we can laud Márcio Thomaz Bastos for choosing so well in his appointment of Chief Paulo Lacerda, I don't believe we can credit the minister with the corporation's success in later years. In fact, the institutional strengthening of the force was due to various factors beyond the will or control of the PT governments or their ministers. Globalization had been underway for at least fifteen years before PT came to power, and the subsequent internationalization of our activities led to an influx of middle-class candidates into the academies, as well as a far higher number of female cadets. Allied with that, the technological revolution, with its rampant advances in terms of communications and other technologies, proved key to an evolution that recast our institution in the light of a changing world. If, one day, institutionalized crime had thought it could control the FP, it was sorely mistaken.

Minister Márcio Thomaz Bastos, PT's arch-consigliere, saw the FP under his indirect command work tirelessly for the good of Brazil and to the despair of the government of which he was a part. There was no stopping the inexorable course this institutional revival had set, particularly because it was coming from four converging fronts all at once: the FP, the public prosecutors' office, the IRS, and the federal courts. None of these was ever going back "into the box." José Eduardo Cardozo must have rued it all as he watched the FP he commanded mortally wound the Dilma Rousseff administration he'd done so much to defend against Operation Car Wash.

The Institutionalization of Corruption

Identifying in PT administrations a deepening institutionalization of crime within the spheres of government does not mean to say that previous administrations were squeaky clean or that we lived in a democracy with no graft. Quite the contrary. Though earlier governments never achieved anything like the centralization and articulation that PT did, they, too, lacked the rectitude or the impetus to combat corruption, and, for that, they ought to be investigated, tried, and punished.

The prior governments were structured somewhat differently. Before the Lula administration, systemic corruption schemes were on a smaller scale, less widespread, and wholesale, though they, too, were highly lucrative, affected the same state-run cash cows, involved the same construction companies, and adopted the same tried-and-tested modus operandi.

Adopting the religious vocabulary of Brazilian politics, the schemes were run out of "churches" by party "cardinals" or small political "sees." They were insular rackets, and the spoils invariably went toward personal illicit enrichment and/or off-the-books campaign funding, but not toward a centralized project of power. The difference was that these schemes were not centralized. There was no clear and direct overseer or holding, controlling things from the Office of the Chief of Staff.

For example, since redemocratization in the 1980s, the MDB had been the largest party in the country in terms of parliamentary seats, but there were two distinct factions. You had the congressional group (led by Michel Temer, Geddel Vieira Lima, Eliseu Padilha, Henrique Eduardo Alves, and, more recently, Eduardo Cunha); and the senatorial group (Renan Calheiros, Eunício Oliveira, Romero Jucá, José Sarney, and others). According to reams of plea-bargain testimony from top brass at companies holding government contracts, these two factions wrestled nonstop, as if they were two separate parties, vying for space in corruption schemes and for juicy posts in the public apparatus.[16]

The PSDB also had its long-standing schisms, especially between the Minas Gerais and São Paulo groups. Operation Car Wash discovered schemes run by both chapters, but, to this day, has never managed to find any overlap between them.

While it would be a mistake to say that this or that party invented corruption in Brazil, it would be just as wrong to attribute the same level of institutionalization to the corruption practiced by the PT administrations and those that preceded them. PT may not have created graft, but it definitely obtained a higher level of efficacy in perpetrating it. The main reasons for that breakdown are as follows:

(1) Direct, proactive centralization and control over the spoils of fraud by the president of the republic's chief of staff;
(2) Supervaluation and turbo-charging of Odebrecht and its enormous capacity to operate in both regular activities and major kickback schemes. The company even adapted its corporate processes to more efficiently accommodate payola;
(3) Exportation of the Brazilian model of corruption through infrastructure construction contracts brokered with other countries in Latin America and Africa, with Odebrecht at the helm;

(4) Harnessing a set of companies, described as "national champions,"
     by granting billion-dollar lines of credit through the Brazilian
     Development Bank (BNDES) and propelling them to market
     dominance while using them as bribe banks for the leaders of
     "allied" parties;
(5) Cementing this model through the marketing skills of the "golden
     couple" João Santana and Mônica Moura, the masterminds
     behind PT's electoral campaigns, and through the burnished
     images of these celebrated "friends" of the new establishment;
(6) The systematic allotment of corruption schemes at state-run or
     state-owned companies to other political parties comprising the
     government's political majority, thus implicating them from top to
     bottom in an overarching criminal project.

Items 3, 4, and 5 make up what we call the "bonanza kit," the complete
package that institutionalized crime on a transnational level by
sponsoring vast infrastructure projects on foreign soil, undertaken
by Brazilian construction companies, financed with credit from the
BNDES and gilded by João Santana's knack for spin and ability to
keep regime-friendly leaders in power. This strategy was deployed in
Cuba, the Dominican Republic, Venezuela, Peru, and some countries
in Africa.

In the words of Police Chief Sérgio Murillo, stationed at Uberlândia,
"it was in this manner that Lula's Chief of Staff 'recast' traditional
corruption in Brazil, taking it to a whole new level and, in the process,
contaminating—or attempting to contaminate—every single institution
it touched." The institutionalized organizational model and fundaments
of their brand of crime bankrolled the party and personal enrichment
followed as a consequence.

Even before Lula rose to power, there were indications that the
national political environment possessed all the ingredients necessary
for the institutionalization of corruption. There were schemes in place
that involved unimaginable sums, such as that at Banestado, the State
Bank of Paraná. Other famous cases were those involving Jorgina de
Freitas, who defrauded the social security system; the bribery scheme at
the Amazon Watchdog Agency (Sivam); the so-called Pink Dossier (graft
used to finance electoral campaigns); scandals concerning kickbacks
on debts and fines in São Paulo; the cases of the regional development
organs Sudam (Amazon) and Sudene (Northeast); and the construction
of the new headquarters of the Regional Labor Court, among countless
others. In São Paulo, there were irregularities concerning the expansion

of the metro system and, in Rio, a so-called Propinoduto (Bribe-pipeline) involving state auditors and tax inspectors.

The approval of a constitutional amendment that allowed President Fernando Henrique Cardoso to run for reelection in 1997 has long been shrouded in accusations of vote-buying. On May 14 of that year, the newspaper *Folha de S. Paulo* ran a story about the existence of a recording in which congressman João Maia of the PFL in Acre claimed to have received 200,000 reais for voting in favor of the amendment. He said the money was paid by then communications minister Sérgio Motta, from the president's PSDB Party, and by the governor of Amazonas, Amazonino Mendes, from his own PFL.[17]

The constitutional amendment came into effect as of the 1998 election, in other words, it changed the rules with the game already underway. Governors and the president elected in 1994, when reelection was not permitted, now had the chance to run for another four-year term.

Worse than the existence of all these scandals was society's incapacity to react as required, demanding punishment. In each case, months of newspaper headlines came to nothing. This inefficiency in dealing with this kind of crime was due, in part, to the degree of politicization of the country's higher courts and the existence of Supreme Court privilege for elected officials.

White-Collar Crime and Webs for Small Insects

The criminal sciences can thank the North American Edwin Sutherland for the expression "white-collar crime." In a celebrated article written in the 1930s, "White-Collar Criminality,"[18] he defined this criminal modality as "a crime committed by a person of respectability and high social status in the course of their occupation." Unlike homicide or armed robbery, white-collar crime can't be committed by just anybody. It requires a special skillset and a superior position in which to misapply it. And make no mistake, white-collar crime causes incomparably more financial damage than any other sort of theft, as the sums moved are colossal.

While the formation we have identified as institutionalized crime in Brazil is, in the proportions it acquired, a phenomenon very specific to our nation, the international literature on criminology does help to give some measure of the degree to which it compromises society and corrodes its institutions. In the same article, Sutherland identified the potential dangers of this type of transgression as follows: "The financial cost of white-collar crime is probably several times as great as the financial cost of all the crimes which are customarily regarded as the 'crime problem.'"

Another interesting aspect broached by Sutherland is the difficulty society has in seeing these crimes as truly injurious. There is often a distorted view in relation to this type of crime. As the perpetrators are apparently "respectable" individuals, such as eloquent politicians or successful businessmen, they tend to be set apart from "the common criminal" and forgiven all too quickly, even after having their improbity amply proven and exposed.

The victims of white-collar crime are not so easy to identify or empathize with, and as the deed is done in air-conditioned offices and the anterooms to government cabinets, these "perps" don't get any blood on their hands—at least not directly. And yet, their actions leave millions of victims in their wake, on under-policed, badly maintained highways, in understaffed, under-equipped hospitals, through all the violence and fatalities that could perhaps have been prevented if the state weren't operating on a shoestring budget because the money these people stole wasn't there when society needed it.

What we see, according to Professor Marcus Fabiano Gonçalves, from the Faculty of Law (Federal Fluminense University), is the myth of danger being spread with all the power of the social imagination and being confronted by the discourse of a critical criminology that, on the other hand, in looking for answers about corruption, tried in vain to reprocess the noble idea of criminal selectivity (of the poor and the Black) as a legal defense favorable to rich, mostly white politicians and businesspeople, supposedly "persecuted" as the causes of immense social damage through institutionalized crime. He also affirms that there is a great deal of interest in keeping the debate on what constitutes a danger to society restricted to the balaclava-wearing, gun-toting image of the street hood (amplified further by sensationalism), seeing as the threat this figure poses eclipses that of the dirty politician, who, by comparison, barely even seems worthy of penal prosecution at all.

When he published "White-Collar Criminality," Sutherland showed how laws and the rules that interpret them are shaped to spare the gangster with the briefcase. It's impossible not to draw an analogy with the Brazilian system today and the sequence of reactions our establishment has deployed against Operation Car Wash.

In 1949, seventeen years after his article on white-collar crime, Sutherland returned to the topic in a second work, in which certain passages seem to be describing our present reality:

The interests of businessmen have shifted to some extent from efficiency in production to the attainment of special privileges from government. This has produced two principal effects. First, it has tended to "pauperize" businessmen, just as poor people who depend on special privileges of welfare organizations are said to be pauperized. Second, it has tended to corrupt government. According to the studies of municipal, state and federal governments made by Lincoln Steffens in the early part of this century, political corruption and graft grow primarily from the efforts of businessmen to secure special privileges. [. . .] Because of the pressure of these businessmen for special privileges, the system of democracy has been changed into control by political bosses and political machines, which is neither representative government nor efficient government, so far as the problems of the general society are concerned.[19]

Sutherland quotes the late nineteenth-century "robber baron" Daniel Drew, when he said: "The law is like a cobweb; it's made for flies and the smaller kinds of insects, so to speak, but lets the big bumblebees break through. When technicalities of the law stood in my way, I have always been able to brush them aside as easy as anything."

Clear evidence that the powers don't move a muscle to rescue the "smaller kinds of insects," while ignoring all the passing wasps, was the Supreme Court's ruling in June 2018 on the use of judicial mandates, provided for in the Brazilian Penal Code of 1941, that compel figures under investigation to turn themselves in for questioning. By a very narrow margin, the court prohibited the practice, which is an important instrument in any police investigation.[20] The grounds for this decision were that summonses of this nature infringe on individual human rights. In a single ruling, a certain cabal within the Supreme Court had dealt a severe blow to the fight against systemic corruption.

Bringing suspects in for questioning (*condução coercitiva* in Portuguese) is a judicial mandate akin to precautionary detention designed to catch figures under investigation on the hop, as it were, before they can destroy evidence or align testimony with codefendants. It enables the police to minimize obstruction ahead of complex operations. The use of the mandate had never bothered the Supreme Court before, so why prohibit it now, just when it was being used to great effect against politicians and major business figures?

Something similar had happened in 2008, when, under the pretense of avoiding "making a spectacle" of prisoners, the Supreme Court prohibited the use of handcuffs. At the time, the minister of justice was Tarso Genro, who even suggested that the Federal Police do up the inside of their holding vans to make them more comfortable. According to Genro, one-time national president of the PT, the vans were "almost inhumane." His request fell on deaf ears. After all, how would it have looked to cushion up the holding vans just because they were carrying a surprising number of politicians and government members of late? These same vans and squad cars had been transporting ordinary criminals for decades and nobody in the ministry seemed to have noticed how hard they were on the backside.

It is clear today that the FP, public prospectors' office, and certain lower-court federal judges had breached the citadel of protection, and that the criminals and their robed guardians were pushing back. In the minds of the old oligarchs of institutionalized crime, the "pact" had been broken. For the corrupt elite, what these federal agents, prosecutors, and judges had dared do was an outrage, an affront, and they were bombarded with accusations for it. One clear expression of this old-school indignation was the threat proffered by one defeated presidential candidate in the 2018 elections, who said that as president, he would put these rogue elements of the justice system "back in their box."

In the book *The Crime Lords: The New Mafias against Democracy*, published in 2003, Jean Ziegler hit upon what one could call a variant of institutionalized crime.[21] Ziegler came very close to our phenomenon when he quotes Eckhart Werthebach, the politician in charge of German counterespionage until 1995:

> For the State of Law, the danger lies not in the criminal act as such, but in the possibility that organized crime should have—due to its vast financial power—the capacity to wield permanent influence on the decision-making processes of democracy. The most immediate and visible consequence of that is the rapid advance of corruption among politicians and others with decision-making power in our society . . . [. . .] Given its colossal financial power, organized criminality secretly amasses enormous and growing influence over the course of our everyday economic, social and political lives, but also over the Justice system and public administration. One day, it will find itself in a position to dictate its norms and values to society [. . .] And with that, we shall see the independence of our Justice system, the credibility of our politicians and public trust in the values and protective power of the State of Law whittle to nothing. That loss of trust and confidence is precisely what [organized crime] wants. What we will be left with, in the end, is a state that is infiltrated, subverted

and even managed by organized criminality. Corruption will then have become an ineluctable and generally-accepted phenomenon.

Werthebach foresaw the hijacking of the state by organized crime, the result of its growing blight upon public power. It is not exactly the same as what we are here describing as institutionalized crime, because it comes from the outside, breaching the cell walls of government and infecting the apparatus, rather than growing within those cells themselves, as a mutation, as in the Brazilian case. The end result—systemic corruption and the vassalization of public administration and justice—is the same, but the source is different. On one hand, we have structured organizations on the fringes of the official system; on the other, a central group born within the core of officialdom, with none of the drawbacks of marginality.

The Brazilian model of institutionalized crime is much more subtle, especially because it is spawned out of political activity, and that's what makes it more difficult to detect and combat. If institutionalized crime proliferated within the legislature, executive, and judiciary, its development and survival depend on the participation of private groups.

Chapter 6

THE INVESTIGATION OF LULA

Corruption has seeped into the fabric and core of certain parties and institutions of the state, becoming, in the process, accepted administrative conduct, degrading the very dignity of politics, and dragging it down to the ignoble level of institutional delinquency.

Celso de Mello, minister of the STF during the trial of Fernando Baiano, indicted under Operation Car Wash

Márcio Anselmo: From whichever angle you approach it, Car Wash can be considered the largest, widest-reaching anticorruption operation in the nation's history. If we take the most prosaic criteria of all—the rank of the authorities under investigation—it was the first under which a former president of the republic was arrested and convicted on corruption charges.

When Lula was deposed for the first time as the defendant in a criminal case, in May 2017, I was no longer among the chiefs of police in charge of the operation. Less than a year beforehand, however, in March 2016, I was on the team that brought him in for questioning under a precautionary-detention mandate and, later, part of the crew that lawfully intercepted an incendiary telephone conversation between the former president and his successor, Dilma Rousseff. That sequence of events had a tremendous, if indirect, bearing on the latter's impeachment from office later that same year.

This was an emblematic chapter in Operation Car Wash. On one hand, because of the symbolic weight of having as its target the man our investigations had identified as the ringleader of the criminal organization that had taken root at the very seat of power. On the other, and perhaps most of all, because the facts of February and March 2016 are the perfect expression of one of the core precepts of what we classify as institutionalized crime: the appropriation of powers of the state to block investigative action. In this case there was a clear attempt to obstruct justice, allied with a flagrant grasp at one of the devices used to ensure chronic impunity in Brazil: Supreme Court privilege.

An Explosive Wiretap

Well into our investigations on this phase of Car Wash, we realized that ex-president Lula didn't have a telephone. Thanks to some earlier tappings and searches, we discovered that the PT leader used a phone that belonged to one of his bodyguards, a man called Moraes.[1] So we put a tap on the guard's number and waited to see if it yielded anything of use to our investigations.

At the time, we were working on three specific cases related to the ex-president, all widely covered in the press. First, the millions of reais received from companies involved in the construction cartel as fees for speaking commitments. And, second and third, suspicions on two counts of concealment and disguise of criminal property, one involving a country retreat in Atibaia, São Paulo, and another concerning a triplex penthouse with an ocean view in Guarujá, offered to Lula by the construction company OAS in place of the far simpler unit his wife, Marisa Letícia, had bought off the plan.

The connection in all three cases was the involvement of construction companies participating in the cartel defrauding public tenders. According to our investigations, the millions of reais in lecture fees, the beachside penthouse, and the entirely made-over country retreat were all payment for the advantages and benefits these companies had received from the Lula government.

Obeying rule number one of all corruption investigations—follow the money—we were able to map the construction companies' outgoings during the periods these properties were under renovation. Our request to lift the secrecy on their banking and financial records was accepted by the courts, but the news leaked, alerting those under investigation and making our job a lot harder.

Finally, our investigation was almost "ripe," which, in police jargon, means the secret phase of the investigation was over and we were ready to take ostensive action, such as filing for search warrants at the residences and companies of those involved.

First, however, we conducted a lawful interception operation on a number of telephones, including the phone we believed Lula was using for his private conversations. Only a couple of days after the wiretapping began, in February 2016, we obtained total assurance that we were on the right track. The device belonging to the bodyguard Moraes was indeed Lula's phone of choice.

Scheduled for March 4, 2016, Operation Aletheia—the Greek word for "reality" or "the search for truth"—became a turning point in

Operation Car Wash. For the first time, Federal Police agents knocked on the door of a former president of the republic with the aim of taking him in for questioning. The plan of action, all authorized by the courts, included the execution of a precautionary-detention warrant. At that juncture, it was essential that we ensured Lula was heard by investigators without any interference, as the phone calls we'd intercepted indicated that attempts were underway to block or obstruct any ostensive moves on the part of the FP.

The early hours of that morning were some of the tensest of the whole operation. I stayed behind at the "base" in Curitiba to help expedite any urgent diligences that might arise. Police Chief Luciano Flores, who was in charge of the investigation into the lecture fees and the renovations of the country retreat and penthouse, was designated to conduct the questioning, largely because of his calm temperament. He had, perhaps, the "coolest head" of the whole team.

It was no ordinary day. Besides the warrants against Lula, we had another ten precautionary detentions to expedite and thirty-three search warrants to execute. As soon as the crews hit the road that morning, something uncanny happened, unseen before or since: our Guardião interception system simply stopped receiving calls.

It was the most crucial moment imaginable, with the teams already en route, and the system inexplicably "crashed" across the whole state of Paraná. We couldn't intercept a single phone call that whole morning. I had to fast-track a judicial request determining that the telephone operators reestablish the interceptions as quickly as possible.

Operation D-day is always bedlam. One team heads for the target, while another stays behind to provide administrative backup and sort out any last-minute surprises. And they do occur. For example, sometimes the address on a warrant turns out to be wrong and has to be corrected by a judge or the individual the warrant has been issued against has just hopped on a flight somewhere that same day. That particular morning was no different.

There was another issue hanging over that operation: the chance of open conflict between demonstrators in favor and against the investigation. Once word got out, groups on either side amassed outside the president's apartment building in São Bernardo do Campo and had to be kept apart by local police. Protests occurred both outside the apartment building and at Congonhas Airport, where Lula was taken for questioning. The agglomeration of rival crowds was a real flash point of the operation, with a clear threat of unrest breaking out in the streets.

As the bodyguard Moraes was not a person of interest, we decided not to confiscate his telephone, because, if we were right, we'd be able to keep the interception running even after the first round of ostensive action.

Our wiretapping revealed that after Lula's precautionary detention, the government started working feverishly to find a way to save him. On the morning of March 16, President Dilma Rousseff committed what we consider to have been the most explicit act of obstruction of justice up to that point: she appointed Lula her new chief of staff. As this is considered a ministerial position in Brazil, it gave Lula Supreme Court privilege and took the investigations against him out of the hands of the lower courts, temporarily at least.

That morning, the president announced that Lula was replacing Jacques Wagner as her chief of staff. It was like a bomb going off. I remember I was having lunch with colleagues at a restaurant we often went to on extremely busy days in Bacacheri, Curitiba, when the message pinged on my phone. It was precisely 1:32 p.m.

The message was from one of the agents working on the interceptions, and he was asking us all to get back to base on the double. Something had just come up on his wiretap. When I arrived, I sat in front of the computer, put the headphones on, and played back the recorded dialogue. I remember it all so clearly, even Tom Jobim's "Ah, se eu pudesse" playing as MOH for a few seconds before the now-infamous exchange between Lula and his successor began:

Dilma: Hello.
Lula: Hello.
Dilma: Lula, let me tell you something.
Lula: I'm listening, dear. Ahn.
Dilma: It's like this, I'm sending Bessias* over to you with a document for you to keep on standby, and use only if necessary. It's your ministerial diploma, ok?!
Lula: Uhum. Okay, okay.
Dilma: That's all, so just wait there, he'll be right over.
Lula: Okay, I'm here, I'll wait.
Dilma: Alright?!
Lula: Alright.
Dilma: Bye.
Lula: Bye, dear.

---

* Jorge Rodrigo Araújo Messias, then deputy chief of legal issues at the Office of the Chief of Staff.

For us, the conversation was ironclad confirmation of the rush to get Lula under the cover of Supreme Court privilege. This was one of the most controversial moments in Operation Car Wash. The ex-president's party claimed the interception had been illegal, because the request that the tap be discontinued had been made before the conversation took place. The request, confirmed in an official dispatch signed by Dilma, was issued precisely because of Lula's appointment to the Office of the Chief of Staff. Judge Sergio Moro, presiding over the case, accepted the request and passed the order on to Police Chief Luciano, who received it around lunchtime that day and immediately gave the order for the telephone operator to cease the interception.

However, anyone who works with lawful interception knows that it takes hours and sometimes even days for the operator to interrupt the monitoring, and it was during this interval that the dialogue between Lula and Dilma was intercepted.

After hearing the conversation, Police Chief Luciano sent a report straight to Judge Moro. In addition, the judge also heard the public prosecutor's office and decided to release the intercepted dialogues. Moro based his decision to do so on Article 5, Item XII, of the constitution, which reads "the secrecy of correspondence and of telegraphic, data and telephone communications is inviolable, except, in the latter case, by court order, in the cases and in the manner prescribed by law for the purposes of criminal investigation or criminal procedural finding of facts."[2]

This was, without doubt, one of the most complex decisions taken during Operation Car Wash, but it was coherent with the general transparency the judge had insisted on from the very beginning. Later on that same day, an extra edition of the *Official Gazette*, published at around 7:00 p.m., gave further proof of the unprecedented rush to sweep the former president into his new post as his understudy's chief of staff. The dispatch ran:

Decree, March 16, 2016

As per the powers invested in her under art. 84, caput, item 1 of the Constitution, the PRESIDENT OF THE REPUBLIC hereby APPOINTS LUIZ INÁCIO LULA DA SILVA to the post of Minister of the President's Chief of Staff.

Brasília, March 16, 2016; year 195 since Independence and the 128th of the Republic. Dilma Rousseff

Publishing an extra edition of the *Official Gazette* was a very unusual procedure and clear indication that the intention was to bulletproof

Lula against further warrants, especially arrest. Extra editions, on the rare occasions they are published, tend to involve urgent normative acts that can't wait until the next day.

The recording in which the president of the republic said she was sending her aide, Jorge "Bessias," with Lula's ministerial diploma, as a sort of "get-out-of-jail-free card," spread like wildfire and was headline news within minutes. By nightfall on March 16, the dialogue was being played through loudspeakers on sound-cars at street demonstrations in various key cities.

In Brasília, crowds of protesters gathered in front of the Presidential Palace. Curitiba was in a state of ebullition, with a throng celebrating outside the federal district court, where Sergio Moro worked. There was not a single parking space to be found within a kilometer radius of the building. The demonstrations went on into the night, with the recording being played as if on-repeat nationwide.

In the meantime, the government stuck to its plan of shielding Lula with Supreme Court privilege. An express swearing-in ceremony was thrown together for the following morning.

In many places during her speech on the occasion, reproduced here, President Dilma Rousseff referred directly or indirectly to the turn of events.

The efficient functioning of the Justice system must rest on the presentation of proof, without conceding its natural preponderance to other instruments; it must rest on constitutional guarantees— and I never tire of repeating this: on citizen's rights and respect for the law. After all, there is no Justice when plea-bargain testimony is made public, selectively, I might add, so that those under investigation can be massacred in the press, and when depositions are transformed into media circuses. There can be no Justice when laws are disrespected—I repeat—and the Constitution is flouted. There is no Justice for the citizenry when the constitutional rights of the president of the republic are violated.

Brazil cannot bow to a conjuration that invades the constitutional prerogatives of the presidency; not because the president is above other citizens; but because, if even presidential prerogatives are offended, what guarantees can the people expect to have?

Concerning the absolutely republican dialogue I maintained with ex-president Lula yesterday, I can only say it was published in a misrepresented form, with verb tenses altered, they even changed "we" to "he," and elided—and I'm keeping this signed document as proof—, elided the fact that what we went to the airport to fetch was president Lula's signature, which is here, signed, but without my signature. And without that this is not a ministerial diploma. President Lula is being sworn in here, now. We're doing this here because president Lula, for personal reasons, would not have been able to attend otherwise, because Maria Letícia [his wife] is unwell. He came here today precisely to show his determination to participate in this government.

So I repudiate, totally and unreservedly, all versions that suggest otherwise. This document was distributed to the press as soon as we realized that this was what it was all about. Now, we are evaluating very carefully the conditions under which this interception was made against the presidency of the Republic. We want to know who authorized it, why, and why it was made public when it contains nothing, absolutely nothing, I repeat, nothing that raises any doubt as to its republican character.

The attempt to save Lula was thwarted the following day. Supreme Court judge Gilmar Mendes suspended the PT leader's appointment on the grounds of "deviation of finality"—in other words, Dilma's real reasons for making the appointment had nothing to do with the work Lula might or might not do in the post but merely to shield him from investigation.

The falsity of aim is quite clear: to prevent an arrest warrant being served by the district court judge. It amounts to an immunity pass issued by the president of the Republic. [. . .] Hovering above the move is the indication that the ex-president would likely be implicated in ulterior investigations, detained on a precautionary basis and criminally charged. Assuming the ministerial post of Chief of Staff would be a concrete form of avoiding such consequences. The conversations intercepted with the authorization of the 13th Federal Court of Curitiba suggest that this was indeed the reason behind the appointment.[3]

The FP's Car Wash team was enormously relieved by the ruling, which was basically a green light for us to continue our investigations. However, the team was divided as to what the next steps should be. For me, what had happened was undeniably an attempt to bar the investigation, so I argued for requesting the ex-president's arrest on charges of obstruction of justice. In my view, that was how the public prosecutor's office ought to proceed in relation to Lula, but I was outvoted.

The decision taken was to send the investigation of the recordings and Lula's appointment to the Supreme Court, which ended up declaring the interception inadmissible in court. Nevertheless, our investigations moved forward.

The Arrest

A little over two years after Lula's precautionary detention, and no longer a member of the original Car Wash team, I was stationed in Brasília when the TRF-4 collegiate court ruled on Lula's appeal against his conviction on a charge of concealment and disguise of criminal property which I had helped build years before.

As the original conviction had been upheld in collegiate court and the sentence extended to twelve years and one month's imprisonment, the original trial judge Sergio Moro issued a warrant for Lula's arrest on April 5, 2018. In deference to the office he'd once held, Lula was given the opportunity to turn himself in, with the assurance that handcuffs would not be used.

However, as soon as the warrant was issued, Lula walled himself up at the HQ of the Steelworkers Union in São Bernardo do Campo, his old stomping ground from back in his days as a union leader, and disobeyed the judge's order. The 5:00 p.m. deadline set for him on April 6, 2018, came and went and still Lula held out. In a flagrant attempt to drum up unrest, the former president continued to claim judicial persecution before a crowd of his most fervent followers. His obvious intention was to force the police to invade the compound in order to arrest him, which would have led to conflict with his grassroots support.

What ensued were lengthy negotiations that culminated, on April 7, in Lula finally agreeing to hand himself over to Federal Police custody—without confrontation. For the first time in the history of the nation, a former president was convicted and jailed for corruption.

Chapter 7

CAPITALISM, THE BRAZILIAN WAY

Everything that is happening is an institutionalized business. It's just how it's always been.[1]

Emílio Odebrecht, during his deposition
to the public prosecutor's office

Márcio Anselmo and Jorge Pontes: At a certain juncture during Car Wash, the team of investigators realized something that, in a sense, summed up the whole operation: a significant percentage of the country's gross domestic product (GDP) was in FP holding cells or jails in Curitiba. The owners and top brass of Brazil's leading construction companies—Odebrecht, Andrade Gutierrez, OAS, UTC—entrusted for decades with building the country's infrastructure, were behind bars.

Rather than cause for commemoration, the general reaction was shock, given the sheer magnitude of the schemes and the sums syphoned off. Even for police agents and prosecutors with decades of corruption investigations under their belts, some of the amounts involved were simply staggering. In 2014, the first year of Operation Car Wash, a gent named Pedro Barusco closed a plea-bargain deal in which he agreed to return no less than $100 million ferreted away into offshore accounts. Barusco was executive manager of services at Petrobras, and despite his power to influence tenders, he wasn't even a director. He was, you could say, middle management.

Odd as it may sound, when it came to executive suspects, the system actually played in our favor. As most of the executives arrested were from private companies, and so enjoyed nothing like the Supreme Court privileges and protections of the politicians, they went to jail sooner and tended to turn earlier.

In other words, the active pole of all this corruption, the business class, was more vulnerable to the march of Operation Car Wash than the mandated officials. The history of the co-optation of public agents by private-sector powerhouses is entirely emblematic of the deterioration of Brazil's democracy. It's also damaging to the functioning of capitalism itself. The promiscuity between private enterprise and public servants deformed free competition and spawned a Brazilian-style corruption based on cronyism and a parasitic thirst for public funds that was prejudicial to the development of more honest companies and indeed that of the nation as a whole.

A symptom of this deformity is the utter corruption of political service into economic activity for the benefit of those members of the legislature and executive willing to act on behalf of the corporations that finance their electoral campaigns. For these individuals, politics is an extremely lucrative line of business. It has become run-of-the-mill for influential politicians to devote their entire mandates to nefarious private interests, pushing through legislation beneficial to certain sectors of industry, championing client companies in public tenders, and securing billion-dollar lines of credit for them from state development banks.

Illustrative of all this is the plea-bargain testimony delivered by Antonio Palocci as part of his deal with the Federal Police, the content of which was made public by the thirteenth District Court of Curitiba. Palocci is very clear: "in nine-hundred of the thousand or so provisional measures[2] issued by PT governments, exotic amendments were exchanged for bribes."

One such instance involved former finance minister Guido Mantega, who is facing charges of corruption and money laundering for his part in securing the approval of Provisional Measures 470 and 472, designed to benefit companies from the Odebrecht Group.[3]

It was crony capitalism all the way, a phenomenon which the American journalist, author, and political consultant Peter Schweizer sees as deriving from a lack of transparency in political systems.[4]

The creation of "national champions" is a classic example of Brazilian cronyism. Under the pretext of fostering important sectors of the economy, the federal government, particularly during the Dilma Rousseff years (2011–16), extended a bevy of benefits and tax breaks to certain companies. Ostensibly, the plan was to help promising concerns rise to dominance in their sectors and so strengthen the national economy and boost competitiveness abroad, but the real intent was to create national titans beholden to the government who would effectively bankroll the election campaigns and personal projects of their political benefactors.

Two particularly glaring recent cases of businesspeople who traded campaign donations for government support were Joesley Batista, from the J&F Group—which became the world's largest animal protein producer—and Eike Batista, who made a fortune in the mining and oil and gas industries. Both were accused of corrupting politicians and spent time behind bars for their crimes. Joesley signed a plea-bargain agreement with the public prosecutor's office in March 2017 and assisted the investigations by secretly recording conversations with key figures, including President Michel Temer. Eike, on the other hand, was handed a thirty-year jail sentence in July 2018 for money laundering and for bribing the former governor of Rio de Janeiro, Sérgio Cabral, in exchange for favorable conditions in his business dealings with the state.[5]

There are also cases of politicians becoming leading businessmen themselves. One such case is the state deputy for Rio de Janeiro Jorge Picciani, who exploited his career as a public official to create one of the largest livestock empires in the country. Between 1998 and 2014, according to *Piauí* magazine, Picciani's personal wealth, as declared to the Electoral Tribunal, grew twentyfold, from half a million reais to 10.4 million. Long a target of Operation Car Wash, Picciani was accused of using his livestock business to launder misappropriated public funds—a charge corroborated by the Rio de Janeiro state auditor, Jonas Lopes.

The misuse of public power invested by the electorate created a new "social class": the nouveau riche of politics, a cabal that amassed vast wealth from the benches of Congress or the cabinets of the nation's ministries and secretariats.

It is redundantly clear that at a crucial point in the construction of the state, Brazil lacked something that was abundant in the United States. Two-hundred and thirty years ago, the founding fathers of the United States, men who knew all too well the weaknesses inherent to human nature, installed the constitutional checks and balances to keep the powers of the republic true to a set of overriding principles, creating in the process a nation in which no one was above the law. On the other hand, when Brazil forged its constitutions—especially the Federal Constitution of 1988—our "floundering fathers" left us with a country stacked entirely in their favor, to the detriment of the rest of the population. These men were, first and foremost, the architects of a disaster waiting to happen. There is no denying the fact that Brazil was designed *not* to function. If we look at it with philosophical objectivity, it was a job well done. We are reaping exactly the effects intended. The design flaws and loopholes that prevent the country from developing and progressing were created by those who benefit from its constant misfiring and inequities.

An Institutionalized Attack on Democracy

In her recent book *Thieves of State*, the American journalist Sarah Chayes explains how kleptocracy can threaten the internal and external security of nation-states. Chayes classifies the different types of corrupt state as follows: the military-kleptocratic complex, bureaucratic kleptocracy, post-Soviet kleptocratic autocracy, and resource kleptocracy.[6]

Chayes' book shows the countries currently in the grips of each variation, but Brazil is best described as a politico-administrative kleptocracy, where politics and the electoral system function as the institutional mainstay of corruption.

What feeds and sustains the flaws and incongruences of our electoral system is the illicit appropriation of public funds by politico-criminal gangs. Though there is no consensus on the best model to adopt, one thing that political scientists and specialists on elections in Brazil are unanimous on is the idea that our system always favors those already in power, facilitating their reelection and, most of all, broadening the influence economic power can exercise on the ballot box.

As the electoral rules are set by Congress, it would perhaps be utopian to expect a political reform that favored parliamentary turnover. The reality, unfortunately, makes it much easier to hold onto a seat than to win one. Brazilian electoral campaigns involve little or no door-to-door canvassing, but rely almost exclusively on media presence (orchestrated campaign marketing) and celebrity endorsements, both of which can be bought. As those already on the inside benefit from lavish illicit campaign funding, they can easily outpunch the pretenders to their seats. Two aspects Operation Car Wash really exposed were the ludicrous amounts of money paid to the top-tier election campaign marketeers (tens of millions of dollars per campaign) and vote-buying, a practice still quite common in Brazil. In 2018, for example, new elections had to be called in sixty-nine Brazilian municipalities because the mayor-elect was found guilty of this brand of electoral fraud.

Institutionalized crime can be seen as a two-pronged attack on democracy. First, by pumping fortunes into the campaigns of its capos, it tilts the electoral playing field in their favor. Second, it directly defrauds the democratic system by using congressional vote-buying to ensure that bills beneficial to institutionalized crime and its donors are passed into law.

In the last two presidential elections, the victorious candidates— Dilma Rousseff in 2014 and Jair Bolsonaro in 2018—ran very different campaigns in terms of costs. In 2014, the former president declared 350 million reais in campaign expenditure, while Jair Bolsonaro spent only 1.7 million.

If we add to that the undeclared contributions, somewhere in the region of 800 million, according to Antonio Palocci, Dilma Rousseff's 2014 campaign cost over a billion reais. In response to Operation Car Wash's revelations on this electoral glut, the Supreme Court banned corporate donations to election campaigns, and though the ruling reduced the sums involved, they still remained high. Fernando Haddad (PT), the defeated candidate in 2018, plowed 34 million reais into his campaign—twenty times more than his adversary, Bolsonaro.

Antonio Palocci's plea-bargain deposition is extremely illustrative on how Brazilian election campaigns were funded:

> For example, the deponent declared that, in return for the major construction contracts granted outside the electoral period, when election time came round again, the directors would repay the political commitment made by negotiating official campaign donations with the treasurers of the parties and coalitions, etc; that even these licit contributions were made using funds of illicit origin; that this was the most common modus, as it was a way of laundering ill-gotten gains with the licit sheen of campaign donations; that it is possible that some official donations did not involve money of illicit origin; that, as such, official campaign contributions sometimes involved both licit and illicit funds, the latter deriving from corrupt dealings; that the electoral court (TSE) had no way of knowing whether or not the donations involved illicit funds, as it does not audit these resources to determine their origin; that most of the contributions declared to the TSE involve illicit funds; that regular accounts can be rendered and approved, yet still involve illicit funding; that PT's main fundraisers were Delúbio Soares, Paulo Ferreira and João Vaccari; that the people encumbered with conducting negotiations with major business figures were the collaborator himself, exclusively during the administration of Luiz Inacio Lula da Silva, and particularly during his [Palocci's] time as a congressman, José Dirceu, and Guido Mantega; that the collaborator never opened offshore accounts in the name of PT or its leaders, but knows that such accounts did exist under other names; that he is aware that business figures opened accounts in their own names exclusively for use by PT; that proof of the illicit nature of the campaigns lies in the extremely high costs involved; that nobody ever makes a campaign

contribution expecting only trivial relations with the future government; that Brazil's electoral law and party political system are highly dysfunctional; that the present investigations, should they continue unencumbered, will reveal themselves unnecessary; that the regular rendering of accounts at the TSE is perfect from a formal perspective, but almost always involves money of illicit origin; that, for example, a campaign costing 500 million reais would be scandalous enough in itself, but becomes even more so in light of the fact that at least 400 million of that importance would certainly be of illicit origin; that the legislation does not work and actually incentivizes corruption; that corruption is occurring more and more within the legal framework itself; that he agrees with the banning of campaign contributions under the current molds, but that implications of this will almost certainly be an increase in off-the-books donations, the inviability of the candidacies of poor people and of professionals receiving advances on professional activities for political purposes; and that PT's presidential campaigns in 2010 and 2014 cost 600 and 800 million reais, respectively.[7]

With the ballot box deformed in this way, it is all but impossible for democracy to exist. What we see take hold here is a cruel logic whereby power is invested in society's assailants by their very victims: the electorate. No matter how hard-fought election campaigns may appear, the real prize is a seat not in the executive or the legislature but at the table of an institutionalized, legally shielded, highly lucrative, and extremely enticing criminal organization.

Elected on the strength of illicit campaign funding, incumbent politicians appoint their cronies to directorates and secretariats with the express purpose of embezzling public funds. Whether by defrauding tenders or padding contracts with the companies that financed their campaigns, vast sums are pilfered from public organs and used to irrigate a complex, deeply embedded mechanism that lines the pockets of politicians, their appointees, and the business figures in cahoots with them. The result is that these companies and corporations make huge profits to the detriment of their competitors and repay their political benefactors in the form of lavish over and under-the-table campaign contributions, to the detriment of their adversaries. It's a symbiotic relationship: everyone on the inside wins; everyone on the outside loses.

There's nothing new in this. Corruption between private concerns and the state dates back to the military dictatorship, when there were no elections to defraud.[8] The decades since re-democratization, and, more recently, the years of economic growth, have certainly inflated the sums involved, while gradually improved investigative policing has made it possible to breach the protective shields of institutionalized crime.

Another damaging consequence of the institutionalization of crime in public/private relations is the fact that society is woefully represented at Congress, state assemblies, and town halls, because candidates to seats thereat are elected on the strength of vigorous injections of dirty money, both on and, more frequently, off the books. That, combined with electoral laws that stack the outcomes in the favor of those in power, means money is the decisive factor in elections, and mandates are spent serving the interests not of those who invested their vote in the chosen candidate but of the donors who spurred him or her to victory in the first place. The end result is more public money filched, more tenders rigged, and more contracts padded. Democracy is nothing more than an illusion when the popular vote is manipulated by a group of powerful businesspeople in the service of institutionalized crime.

The municipal elections of 2016 were the first to reveal the impact of Operation Car Wash and the prohibition of corporate campaign donations. Compared with earlier campaigns, expenditure was significantly lower.

Another effect is that the money allotted through the Special Fund for Financial Assistance to Political Parties has attained a whole new relevance in the post-ban environment. As the size of the allotment depends on the number of seats held by each party, unscrupulous seat-holders can basically sell their affiliation to the highest bidder. In the months of March and April 2018, for example, in the buildup to elections, the Brazilian Congress and state assemblies transformed into Persian markets. The so-called party transfer window, the only time of the year when mandated officials can switch parties without censure, became a free-for-all of haggle and carrot-dangling. In an attempt to poach seat-holders from their rivals, party presidents promised lavish budgets for reelection campaigns, among other goodies, in an all-out bidding war. In February 2018, the *Folha de S.Paulo* newspaper ran a piece in which members of various parties remarked, off-the-record, and in a tone of dismay, that "the wheeling-and-dealing ha[d] never been so explicit," "ideology doesn't come into it; it's all about money." Congressman for the state of Mato Grosso, Nilson Leitão (PSDB), complained that members of his party were being indecently propositioned left, right, and center: "I said straight out: 'If any of you wants to leave because of money, then good riddance.'"

Off-the-books campaign funding won't disappear, especially not while the ban on official corporate contributions holds, but less money is certainly circulating under the table since Operation Car Wash. It's a prophylactic reflex of the punishments meted out to the biggest donors during those most active years, many of whom are now in jail or facing the very real prospect of ending up there.

The Orient Express Effect

Many of the major police operations that have tried in recent years to break the link between public and private share a focus on tender fraud. The main challenge facing the FP today is to sharpen its ability to identify this type of crime. It's not easy, but it is certainly urgent. Crime grows more sophisticated by the day, and it's no exaggeration to say that investigations dealing with other forms of crime have become very straightforward by comparison with those tackling public procurement fraud.

What we can see is that criminals involved in defrauding public procurements do not even desist from the practice when under investigation. Unlike cases of drug trafficking, for example, where the perpetrators lie low as soon as they realize the police are onto them, those committing procurement fraud tend to occupy positions that give them the means to cover their tracks, even under a watchful eye. Investigation does not deter them.

In general, all those involved in these schemes are on the same page: the companies awarded the contracts; those who submit the losing bids, just to make a show of competition; the public agents in charge of awarding the contracts; the politicians who appointed them and their intermediaries. Having all these parties working together makes the investigation more difficult and the malleability of the criminal organization all the greater. If, for instance, the initial agreement was to deposit a sum in the account of a partner or relative of one of those involved, or to send the money to an account in the principality of Liechtenstein, the move is merely suspended until something more secure can be found—something not yet on the authorities' radar. But the crime itself, the arrangement, the padded pricing, the spreadsheet acrobatics, the collusion between the beneficiary and the false bidders, the leaking of the requirements for the winning bid, the participation of the public administrator who requisitions the procured good or services, all of this goes on as agreed. In other words, the rigged bid is just a show, a pantomime that looks convincing enough to those who don't know what's going on behind the scenes.

All the participants in the scheme play their part in landing the same pernicious result, so there is no weak leak in the chain. Some call it the "Orient Express effect," after the Agatha Christie novel in which all the suspects—passengers on a train—are guilty of the same murder, each having stuck the knife into the victim.

It's a strategy that has always contributed toward Brazil's history of impunity, and so it is easy to understand the immense public support investigations into these schemes, particularly Car Wash, have received since the outset. The possibility of finally convicting the nation's untouchables, the rich and the powerful of business and politics, has turned much of the population into rapt observers of the investigations and of the judicial process as a whole.

One of the most fruitful attacks, in terms of evidence-gathering and proof of how the mechanism worked, was Operation Sand Castle (Castelo de Areia), an earlier version of Lava Jato, launched in 2009. The FP found proof of corruption and contract-padding by the construction company Camargo Corrêa. Four of the construction giant's executives and one money-mover were arrested, and evidence was obtained concerning bribe payments to politicians from no fewer than seven political parties (DEM, PMDB, PP, PSDB, PPS, PDT, and PSB).

It was the same modus operandi laid bare by Car Wash, in which Camargo Corrêa would reappear years later, particularly in relation to the massive sums skimmed off the construction of the Abreu & Lima oil refinery in Pernambuco, a construction project already in the crosshairs of the 2009 investigation. But the system was stronger back then and Sand Castle was annulled by the Superior Court of Justice (STJ) in 2011 on the baffling grounds that investigations could not be based on anonymous tip-offs. The court threw out key wiretap recordings along with the whole body of evidence gathered by the operation. It was Operation Faktor all over again.

The cartel building discovered by Operation Car Wash reached such a degree of smug pseudo-officialdom that a document was drawn up enumerating the "League Rules." Defrauding public tenders at Petrobras was no Viking raid. There was a book of regulations, and Operation Car Wash obtained a copy of the document as part of the collaboration agreement with Augusto de Mendonça Neto, an executive from one of the cartel's member companies, Toyo Setal. Written as if referring to a sports league, article one of the rules reads: "These are the regulations for an annual championship with the participation of sixteen clubs which will play against each other and third parties. A prize, defined here as a 'Trophy,' will be awarded to the winner of each round."[9]

The objectives were evident: "The championship is designed to prepare the teams to compete in domestic and international competitions, with the aim of breaking records and obtaining ever larger prizes." The rules were also clear: "It is imperative that there be [. . .] sound judgement and mutual trust, i.e., one and all must be committed to the competition and serve as its guarantors."

Further on in the "regulations" comes the following stipulation: "The table should be drawn up for a biannual period at least, subject to updates in the event of changes and/or the addition of new fixtures. A trio of directors will be elected to ensure these updates are made accordingly." "No fewer than six teams must compete in each round, and their participation must be extremely active and competitive."

Elsewhere in the "regulations" obtained by the operation the rules are repeated under the title "Sport Club 'United We Stand'": "Sport's players will accept a minimum participation of 60% of the prize money paid per Regional Federation game and 40% per National League fixture, considering all local fees and percentages payable to their opponents in each case."

Further on it is written: "Players can select their games of preference, taking into consideration where they would be best equipped to help Sport Club to victory."

Rain Hours

When they can no longer plausibly deny the facts, cartel members and their executives tend to "play the victim," insinuating or outright claiming that they were corralled, blackmailed, corrupted against their will, forced to play along or go bust, given their reliance on public contracts.

The cycle usually begins with an attempt to influence or even "buy" judicial rulings to shelve the investigations. In parallel, the companies refuse to admit any wrongdoing, but when this ceases to be a viable course of action, they paint themselves as victims railroaded by corrupt politicians. This particular approach was present in many of the public "apologies" the corporations unmasked by Operation Car Wash found themselves forced to make. On December 1, 2016, Odebrecht published a note under the title "Odebrecht apologizes for its mistakes," which began as follows:

> Odebrecht acknowledges its participation in illicit actions in its business activities.
> It does not matter that we gave in to external pressure. Nor is it relevant that there are behaviors that the private and public sectors must resist and correct in their relationships.[10]

Besides the mild wording, adopting "illicit actions" instead of "crimes," this was not a question of merely "giving in to external pressure." The "behaviors" that ought to be resisted and "corrected" were, in fact, a win-win situation, not a case of the former being strong-armed into something beneficial to the latter alone. At the end of the day, the money that oiled the mechanism came straight out of the public coffers and into everyone's pockets, on both sides of the equation.

Over the course of the various investigations we took part in down through the years, we learned a number of inventive ways the price of a construction job can be padded, but an audit by the Federal Court of Accounts (TCU) discovered one ruse that was surprising even by Brazilian standards: compensation for "rain hours." An addendum was written into contracts to determine that Petrobras would compensate the consortium engaged to construct the Abreu e Lima oil refinery for periods during which their machinery was unable to function due to inclement weather. These "rain hours" were often priced way above normal hours worked. In other words, it was a way of padding the contract by making downtime even more lucrative to the construction companies than billable hours. In 2017, the TCU recommended that Petrobras annul this addendum.

In light of all the evidence amassed, there is simply no buying the thesis of the well-intentioned businessman railroaded by corrupt politicians, and when threatened with jail time, it seldom takes executives long to disclose the real scheme of things and their far from passive role in it. In fact, plea-bargain testimony from countless executives has shown that many of these generous corporate campaign donors lorded it over their congressman and senators, who bent over backward to do their bidding when it came to pushing through beneficial legislation. Of course, the same replicated at state assemblies and city halls nationwide.

It's pointless trying to play chicken-and-egg with the origin of public/private corruption in Brazil, asking with whom the "original sin" lies—unscrupulous public managers or bribe-toting businessmen. In his plea-bargain depositions in December 2016, Emílio Odebrecht admitted that the group had been bribing officials since back in his father's day, in the 1940s. Both sides of the counter had always been happy with how things went, so nothing was ever done to question it or change it. As one collaborator joked: "If you look hard enough, you'll find bribe payments as far back as the Lei Áurea."[11]

There is no more eloquent example of just how satisfying this quid pro quo was for both sides than Odebrecht's creation of a department with the sole remit of organizing bribe payments to public agents. The Structured Operations Department was the institutionalization of bribery in the most brazen form possible, normalizing malfeasance as if it were just another aspect of the business. It has become an academic case study in corporate criminality, the clearest-ever expression of the private facet of institutionalized crime.

The FP's discoveries, plus the content of depositions by money launderers, leave no doubt that corruption was always in the company's DNA. While the Structured Operations Department is the most rounded example of systemized corruption, the Odebrecht Group is far from being the only enterprise to refine the practice. Other construction giants not only honed their ways of breaking the law but worked together to do it. In addition to the fraud itself, the manipulation of public procurement tenders has another deleterious effect: the cartel blocks out other companies not willing to play the game.

Lastly, it is important to underscore that this institutionalized approach topples once and for all the old excuse that these companies were victims of corrupt public officials: if they could pull together to set padded prices and rig tenders, they could just as easily have teamed up to resist these supposed extortions and to denounce the improper overtures to the federal authorities. Something that never happened.

With the inner workings of the companies investigated by Operation Car Wash brought to light, many of them announced the adoption of a string of governance practices they had never respected before—a package of virtuous measures known as "compliance," conformity with the law and internal and external codes of ethics.

Compliance became a buzzword in Brazilian corporate speak, but until only a short time ago, it was totally ignored in practice by business interests and public agents alike. Law 12,846/13, known as the Anti-Corruption Law, put the private sector at the heart of the matter, beholden to a set of norms designed not only to prevent corruption but also to encourage the adoption of ethical conduct.

Ridding the marketplace of corruption has become a core responsibility of corporate environments. It is infinitely less harmful and expensive to avoid committing this type of crime than it is to be held accountable for its effects. In short, those who invest in compliance won't need to pay a thousandfold more to clean their name afterward. Vaccination, in this case, is far better than cure.

Another argument those under investigation often trotted out was that an all-out attack on the companies responsible for building and maintaining the country's infrastructure could "break" the economy. It was, in effect, a variant of the "too big to fail" mentality. But, as Judge Sergio Moro liked to say, it is also tantamount to laying the blame for the murder on the person who found the corpse.

In addition to syphoning off badly needed resources which the government could have saved or invested in other areas, the formation of oligopolies and cartels is a crime against the economy and against capitalism itself. The hope is that laying bare the corrupt relations between the private and public sectors can usher in a new age of respect for the law across the Brazilian economy as a whole.

The East African leader and thinker Augustine Ruzindana presided over Uganda's Public Accounts Committee before becoming an activist and consultant at Transparency International. In his essay "The Importance of Leadership in Fighting Corruption in Uganda," he established five devastating effects corruption has on national economies: (1) corruption leads to economic waste and inefficiency, (2) corruption contributes to the persistence of underdevelopment and poverty in countries that are richly endowed with natural resources, (3) corruption exacerbates poverty by stunting development, (4) corruption is an impediment to foreign investment and foreign assistance, and (5) corruption distorts official decisions.[12]

All five of the deleterious effects identified by Ruzindana are present in Brazil and with ever deeper impact. Over the last decade, institutionalized crime found fertile ground in which to thrive, thanks to global growth, commodities booms, and record tax receipts. The influx of tens of millions of Brazilians into the middle class and the subsequent rise in consumption meant there was more money than ever to tap into, and opportunity, as the saying goes, makes the thief.

Institutionalized crime rose and spread, purloining vast amounts of money set aside for infrastructure development. The targets of choice are almost always companies in the energy, mining, oil and gas, electricity, and nuclear sectors, as well as the revenue services and tax inspection.

The formula, as ascertained, is to defraud public procurement processes by awarding padded contracts on construction work and services.

It would be dramatic enough to see public works made substantially more expensive by corruption in a country with widespread poverty and serious infrastructure problems without the added perversion of having such colossal projects make it off the drawing board solely in order to feed the already bloated vampires of the state and private sector. By way of recent example, not only was 211 million reais skimmed off the renovation of Rio's Maracanã Stadium ahead of the Olympic Games and FIFA World Cup in 2014 (former governor Sérgio Cabral was convicted of receiving bribes on this deal) but an entirely unnecessary stadium was built from scratch in São Paulo, already home to the massive Morumbi and Alianz stadiums, and others in Brasília and Manaus, which do not even have a single first-division football team between them, merely as opportunities for further corruption. In fact, over half of the stadiums built or renovated for the 2014 World Cup are under investigation for irregularities.[13] Such was the hunger for graft within the federal government and among its allies that shining white elephants were built to make sure that everyone got a slice of the action.

The argument that it was important to tread softly so as not to hobble the national economy earned the construction cartels lenient treatment and soft plea-bargain deals with the state. But we have to ask: What would have been the fairest punishment for these companies? And how would they have been dealt with in other countries?

Many argue that we have to punish the people, not the companies. But what about corporations that have continued with the same criminal practices despite changes in command over the decades? We might imagine that in countries with more rigid anticorruption legislation, these companies would not have found it quite so easy to go on operating outside the law.

On the other hand, we also see multinationals that normally act within the law start to dance to the local tune as soon as they set up operations in Brazil, handing out bribes to government authorities without a second thought. In *Corruption and Government*, Susan Rose-Ackerman, professor of jurisprudence at Yale University, and Bonnie J. Palifka, professor at the Instituto Tecnológico y de Estudios Superiores, Monterrey (ITESM), claim that "all too often, reputable multinational firms find themselves facing the 'prisoner's dilemma' when operating in corrupt regimes."[14] "Each believes it needs to pay bribes in order to do business, but also knows it would be better for everyone if no-one did."[15]

The Noncrime

In the 1930s and 1940s, Sutherland analyzed 980 court decisions against the 70 largest manufacturing, mining, and mercantile corporations in the United States and found that, even though it was ruled that the companies had acted unlawfully in every single case, in only 158 of these—a little over 15 percent—was the offense committed considered, and sentenced, as criminal conduct.

On this point, the author asked: Why don't criminologists treat white-collar crime like any other?[16] And the answer returns to the stigma of criminality, which does not seem to stick to this kind of malfeasance. Sutherland is clear: "Violations of these laws, to be sure, do not call forth as much resentment as do homicide or rape, but not all laws in the penal code involve equal resentments by the public."[17]

What we have seen in Brazil over the years is no different. On countless occasions, members of the "political class" have promptly come to the defense of criminal companies, again, on the grounds of preserving the economy. It has been almost impossible to get businesspeople or public agents convicted of crimes to recognize themselves as criminals. Bribery, for example, has gone by all sorts of euphemisms—commission, consulting fees, par-for-the-course, plus fees, and so on—called anything except by its own name.

In our case, it was years into Operation Car Wash before the construction company executives and government agents began to see themselves as criminals, but even then, and despite the considerable body of evidence against them, many refused others to own up to their criminality and see it for what it was.

Once again, Sutherland's conclusions on the deleterious effects of this practice, penned almost a hundred years ago, sound more current now than ever:

> While businessmen state that they are simply trying to avoid the excesses of competition, it is precisely these excesses—the cut-throat attribute of competition—which regulated the system, according to the earlier economists. For free competition as the regulator has been substituted a private collectivism, in which the public is not represented, and in which the public receives little consideration. This system of private collectivism is very similar to socialism, except that it does not include representation or consideration of the public.
>
> Businessmen have also been active in restricting the principle of free enterprise. Although businessmen have been vociferous as

to the virtues of free enterprise and have insisted, in general, that government keep its hands out of and off business, businessmen above all others have put pressure on government to interfere in business. They have not done this en masse, but as individuals or small groups which have been endeavoring to secure a preferential advantage.[18]

And so persists the systemic logic of self-protection from the letter of penal law, blowing a bubble around these criminals, who remained, for years on end, unwilling to shoulder their responsibilities. At the same time as they bray against state intervention in the economy, they secretly bask in the benefits of a system that protects their status and market dominance.

Chapter 8

JEWELRY, RACKETEERS, AND BAD CHECKS—A STATE ON THE RAMPAGE

What's happening at Petrobras happens Brazil-wide: with highways, railways, ports, airports, hydroelectric stations.

Paulo Roberto Costa, former supply chain director at Petrobras, during a congressional hearing on the Petrobras investigations

Jorge Pontes and Márcio Anselmo: Brasília is the seat of power, but in the national imagination it is also a cesspit of political wheeling-and-dealing and nefarious relations between the public and private sectors. Small wonder, given the decades-long string of scandals at the heart of successive federal governments. But Brazil is a federation, and on the state level, Rio de Janeiro, the former national capital, is the perfect example of a system of government entirely debased by institutionalized crime.

Cabral's Rio—Mega-Events and Mega-Corruption

Launched in 2016, Operation Calicute (Calcutta), the Rio chapter of Car Wash, revealed the near-caricatural extent to which former governor Sérgio Cabral's administration embodied all the components of a "textbook" case in institutionalized crime: endemic corruption within the executive, procurement fraud rife across the board, bribes paid to private companies and elected officials as standard practice, state auditors appointed to their posts in order to cover tracks and lend a gloss of probity, and so on.

In Rio de Janeiro, Sérgio Cabral reproduced to the letter the model of institutionalized malfeasance installed at federal level during the administrations of Lula and Dilma Rousseff. As with the *mensalão* congressional retainers paid by PT during Lula's first term of office, and the Petrolão scheme installed and operated throughout PT's thirteen years in power, Cabral pervasively corrupted two of Rio's three powers, the executive and legislature. Police Chief Antonio Carlos Beaubrun, Jr., one of the FP authorities who coordinated Operation Car Wash in Rio, said that Calcutta quickly ascertained the sheer reach of Cabral's corruption: he profited from every single aspect of his government, from health to transport, public works to prison meals.

Operation Calcutta was named after the Indian city where the "discoverer" of Brazil, Pedro Álvares Cabral, suffered a major defeat in 1500, at the hands of Hindus and Muslims eager to retain their monopoly over trade in the region. He lost ships and a lot of men in a battle known as the "Storm of Calcutta." Five-hundred and sixteen years later, thanks to joined dots and a dose of chance, his namesake Sérgio was about to face a storm of his own, only this time the charge was led by the Federal Police.

Three previous investigations paved the way toward this offensive against corruption in Rio. First, Operation Car Wash, based in Paraná, discovered a corruption scheme involving the construction of the Angra 3 nuclear plant by Eletronuclear, a subsidiary of the state electricity company Eletrobras. Contracts with Andrade Gutierrez and other construction companies were padded for kickbacks to various public agents, including the former chairman of Eletronuclear, Othon Luiz Pinheiro da Silva, sentenced to forty-three years in prison in 2016 on counts of corruption, money laundering, and criminal association.

In October 2015, Supreme Court judge Teori Zavascki, rapporteur of Operation Car Wash at the STF, decided that this particular case was not directly related to Petrobras—and so not under the jurisdiction of Sergio Moro's thirteenth District Court in Curitiba. The case was thus transferred to the seventh District Court in Rio de Janeiro, under the responsibility of a then little-known federal judge named Marcelo Bretas.

Three months earlier, in June, Bretas had authorized another operation—Saqueador (Raider)—which ended up uncovering a money-laundering scheme involving public contracts awarded to the construction company Delta. Among those arrested at the time were Delta's owner, Fernando Cavendish, the racketeer Carlinhos Cachoeira, former Delta director Cláudio Abreu, and the lobbyists Adir Assad and Marcelo José Abbud. All told, between 2007 and 2012, Delta had landed public contracts worth eleven billion reais. The scheme revealed by Operation Saqueador consisted in the embezzlement of large chunks of this bonanza through fictitious subcontracts awarded to paper companies. Cavendish, it turns out, was a personal friend of Sérgio Cabral. A lavish but ultimately tragic birthday party held for the Delta owner on the Bahia coast in 2011 revealed the extent of the proximity between the governor of Rio and one of the greatest beneficiaries of construction contracts with the state. A helicopter flying guests to the resort where the celebrations were to be held crashed into the ocean, killing the girlfriend of Sérgio Cabral's son and Cavendish's wife, Jordana Kfuri. The governor and the businessmen were to take the next flight up to Bahia in the same chopper.

As the investigations into the Delta contracts gathered momentum, Cabral initially tried to deny any relationship with Cavendish. When that didn't stick, he rolled out the State Administrative Code of Ethics— of his own authorship—which regulated relationships between state government authorities and the private sector. Article 10, Item ii of this code, forbids civil servants from receiving "gifts, transport, hospitality, compensation or any other favors, or to accept invitations to lunches, dinners, parties and other social events" from companies or their representatives. As an assiduous user of the private jet belonging to the millionaire businessman Eike Batista, Cabral was an inveterate violator of his own code. No other politician embodied quite so cartoonishly the promiscuity that exists between Brazil's political and business classes, as was amply demonstrated by the sixteen criminal suits Cabral faced, the nine convictions these yielded, and the two centuries of jail time he was sentenced to serve (198 years and 6 months, to be exact).

The third point that teed up Operation Calcutta was hatched, like the Eletronuclear case, down south in Curitiba. Operation Car Wash had the cartel of major construction companies in its crosshairs and some of their top executives, faced with the body of evidence against them, decided to cut deals.

Regarding Cabral, the testimony of the directors of the construction giant Andrade Gutierrez proved particularly damaging. Clóvis Primo and Rogério Nora de Sá told investigators that the former Rio governor habitually charged 5 percent on every construction contract awarded during his administration, and the examples they gave included the renovations of Maracanã Stadium ahead of the World Cup in 2014, to the cost of over one billion reais, and the construction of the Metropolitan Ring Road.[1] The modus operandi in Rio was the same as that used on the federal level, with cartels formed to defraud public tenders through rigged bids. It was as a special favor to Cabral that Cavendish's company was included on the Maracanã job, as the winning consortium— Andrade Gutierrez and Odebrecht—had already been decided.

In his deposition before a federal judge, Cavendish admitted that Delta's inclusion was payback for a gift the businessman made, at Cabral's request, to the former First Lady of Rio de Janeiro, Adriana Ancelmo. On a trip the two friends took to Monaco in 2009, the governor asked Cavendish to buy a present for his wife—and it wasn't just any present but a diamond ring with a six-figure price tag. On December 4, 2017, during a deposition before Judge Marcelo Bretas, Cavendish related the episode as follows:

> I knew Odebrecht was favorite to land the Maracanã contract. I visited Governor Cabral [. . .] and told him I was interested in taking part. He agreed with Delta coming aboard, and that's where the ring story becomes relevant. Three months earlier, we were traveling together: me, my wife, the governor and Adriana, whose birthday fell during the trip. We were near Nice, in some small town on the coast, and he took me to a jewelry store. He said he wanted to get something for Adriana, and then he turns to me and says: "I would like you to pay for it." It struck me as an unusual request, for sure, as it was quite a considerable sum, 220 thousand Euro. So I said, alright, I'll pay and we can settle it later. I made it clear it wasn't just a gift from me.[2]

Cavendish continued his deposition by explaining how the ring was basically a bribe paid in advance for Delta's slice of the Maracanã contract:

> Months later, the Maracanã job was Cabral's chance to settle the tab. I asked, and he got Delta in. He also demanded a 5% cut on Delta's earnings on the job, and I deducted the sum [paid for the ring] from that. The ring never was a gift, and if the ex-governor says it was, he's lying. It wasn't a present, it was business.

The amount of jewelry seized among the assets of Sérgio Cabral and Adriana Ancelmo stunned the police. Antonio Beaubrun, one of the FP chiefs who took part in two search and seizure operations at the couple's apartment, said he was taken aback to find yet more jewelry on the second search. Staff claimed they were just trinkets of no real value, but Beaubrun, who had seized a whole treasure trove of jewelry on the first search, took the new swag away for valuation. When the report came back, the estimated value was a whopping million reais, further proof that Cabral and his wife had been laundering money through expensive jewelry and continued to do so even under investigation. And, as Cavendish said, it was all a lot more than just gifts.

Delta's participation in the cartel that benefited from fraud under Cabral's administration proved key to sealing the former governor's fate. Thanks to this connection, the Superior Court of Justice decided that the investigations into Delta's crimes in Rio were connected with those the company was being investigated for under Operation Saqueador. That meant both cases stayed in the hands of Judge Marcelo Bretas, who took a consistently tough line on white-collar crime.

The final element that helped topple Cabral was actually a strategic misstep on his part, and it helps show that minor details can be the undoing of major corruption schemes in a country where the laws are often written to protect those who break them. One of the legal prerogatives most beneficial to criminal authorities is Supreme and superior courts privilege. The higher courts, stocked with judges appointed by the executive, are not only more lenient toward corrupt politicians but much, much slower in its deliberations.

In the first semester of 2014, Operation Car Wash was only getting started. In April that year, Sérgio Cabral had resigned from his gubernatorial post so that his vice and successor, Luiz Fernando Pezão, could gain visibility ahead of the upcoming elections in October. Cabral's approval ratings had tanked since the previous year, when he was one of the prime targets eviscerated by crowds during the June 2013 protests.[3] To the surprise even of his allies, he decided not to run for office in 2014. It was a fatal miscalculation. As a two-term governor, if he had run for Congress, for example, he would almost certainly have won a seat and therefore maintained superior court privilege.

However, by declining to run, Cabral made himself a target of Operation Car Wash in the years that followed. In June 2016, with the discoveries Operation Saqueador brought to light, particularly through the Andrade Gutierrez plea-bargain depositions, a joint public prosecutors' office and Federal Police task force were set up in Rio de Janeiro. In November that year, prosecutors had already built such a substantial case against Cabral that they were able to file for a warrant for his arrest. The FP came knocking on Cabral's door in the swanky Leblon neighborhood on the morning of November 17, 2016. Operation Calcutta was underway.

The Rio chapter of Car Wash was a textbook case of what can be achieved when the public prosecutors' office and Federal Police do their jobs correctly and the courts refuse to shield the powerful. It kickstarts a virtuous cycle that makes it far easier to get to the bottom of crimes. In December 2016, a month after Cabral was arrested without bail, two brothers paid a visit to the public prosecutors in Rio. They were Marcelo and Renato Chebar, and it was the first time the Calcutta task force had heard of either.

The Chebar brothers introduced themselves as financial operators—money-movers—in the employ of Sérgio Cabral. They informed the prosecutors that they had moved over $100 million for the former governor, in both Brazil and abroad, mostly through offshore accounts in their own names. Seeing Cabral, the leader of Rio's white-collar mafia, sent down, the brothers decided it was only a matter of time before they were caught in the operation's net and that it would be better to cut a deal while they still could—and would—in January 2017. The Chebars presented ample material evidence, including bank statements and account numbers, that opened conducive new lines of investigation.

After that, and with further evidence coming from other lines of enquiry, what ensued was the avalanche that transformed Operation Calcutta into such a unique case in the history of anticorruption investigations in Brazil. The Cabral years will go down in history as the period during which Rio's state administration was vitiated through and through by a criminal organization. The evidence amassed permits only one conclusion: under Cabral the embezzlement of public funds became institutionalized as standard practice across the board.

Offshoots from the main investigation revealed the arsenal of ways the government employed to filch state resources. In March 2017, Operation Tolypeutes brought to light the corruption scheme behind the construction of Rio's Linha 4—Amarela subway line, the most expensive public construction project undertaken by the state during the period. The line connects Rio's south zone with the upscale Tijuca neighborhood on the west side. The operation was named after the tunneling animal *Tolypeutes tricinctus*, the three-banded armadillo, incidentally the critter adopted as the 2014 World Cup mascot.

The following month, Operation Fatura Exposta (Exposed Invoice) blew the lid off a scheme to defraud the health department. Cabral's health secretary, Sérgio Côrtes, colluded with the importer Miguel Iskin to pad contracts for the provision of hospital equipment and medical supplies.[4] The fraud had been underway since Côrtes' time as director of the National Institute of Traumatology and Orthopedics (INTO), so it was a case of the same scam transposed from federal to state level.

While corruption involving departments with massive budgets, such as health and transport, are practically a Brazilian "tradition," no cookie jar was safe under Cabral, no matter how small. In June 2016, Operation Ratatouille exposed the shady gubernatorial relations of another businessman, Marco Antônio de Luca. According to the evidence obtained, de Luca had been paying bribes to Cabral in return for contracts for the provision of meals to the state's schools and prisons.[5]

Cabral's institutional kleptomania spared no budget under his care, from the debilitated, understaffed, and under-equipped health system to the contents of the schoolkids' lunch boxes. In contrast with the abject poverty found in swaths of Rio de Janeiro, the ramshackle state of public hospitals, the crime ravaging the shantytowns and streets of the capital, and the penury of the state universities, Cabral lived like a king at the taxpayer's expense, using state-operated helicopters to fly his family and their pet dog off to their lavish beachside mansion in Mangaratiba. In all, there were 1,039 flights between Rio and the gated community on the Costa Verde. Add to that the governor's bike trips around Paris, dinners at some of the French capital's most expensive restaurants, and his tailored Italian suits, and you have the very picture of a man who saw elected office as an opportunity for personal enrichment and nothing else. The assurance of impunity extended to people of his standing by Brazil's dysfunctional and lenient penal system emboldened Cabral to steal, but he was nowhere near as untouchable as he'd once thought. Today, he is serving time in a state prison which he inaugurated himself while governor.

In October 2017, Calcutta revealed the international face of the group's incessant graft. Based on information provided by the Chebar brothers, Operation Unfair Play, launched on October 5, exposed the payment of bribes to members of the International Olympic Committee (IOC) in 2009 in exchange for key votes that helped land Rio de Janeiro the 2016 Olympic Games. The investigation was further buttressed by a collaboration request from French authorities, which had identified unusual payments to then president of the International Association of Athletics Federations—IAAF, Lamine Diack.

According to bank statements obtained by the investigators, the Senegalese official and his son, Papa Diack, received two million dollars from Cabral to buy as many as nine votes. The operation led to the temporary imprisonment of the chairman of Brazil's Olympic Committee, Carlos Arthur Nuzman.[6] Nuzman, who mediated the bribes for Cabral, claimed that there was no crime to investigate, as the IOC is a private body, and Brazil's anticorruption legislation only considers illicit payments made to public agents. The investigators, on the other hand, counterargued that the cash used to bribe the IOC members was public money, and bribery charges were brought against the chairman and Cabral on October 19, 2017.[7]

It was a highly symbolic case. Though the sum involved was small by comparison with most of the bribes revealed by Car Wash and other branches of the operation, the choice of Rio de Janeiro as Olympic City provided a gushing fountain of opportunity for kickbacks and scams of the most varied forms. By way of illustration, even the lines of credit extended to companies involved in the revitalization work on Rio's Port Zone, the flagship project of Rio's Olympic makeover, were infected with graft. Directors at the Caixa Econômica Federal, a retail and development bank that acts as an implementing agency for government projects, demanded bribes in order to release the funds. According to testimony by former Caixa director Fábio Cleto, companies that wanted their funding sooner rather than later had to pay a fee to Cleto and disgraced centrist politician Eduardo Cunha, a former Speaker of the Lower House.[8]

It was also a clear expression of just how deteriorated the three levels of public administration had become in Brazil. At the announcement of the new host city in Denmark, on October 2, 2009, before the eyes of the world, Governor Sérgio Cabral, President Luiz Inácio Lula da Silva, Olympic Committee chairman Arthur Nuzman, and the mayor of Rio, Eduardo Paes, jumped up and down, hugged and punched the air in triumph. It was Rio's golden moment, yet it was, as we would soon see, secured by bribes paid with public money. Though Lula and Paes were not directly implicated in the vote-buying, it is noteworthy that the former Rio mayor was the only member of the party not to have since been jailed for corruption.

The reasons behind the raucous celebrations in Copenhagen were likely quite different to those that drew crowds to Copacabana Beach that same day. In the moral quagmire Brazil's recent governments have bequeathed, it's certainly no overreach to assume that the major sporting events Brazil hosted in the 2010s, including the 2014 World Cup, with its twelve stadiums priced for kickbacks, were nothing but opportunities for institutionalized crime.

Another ramification of Operation Car Wash in Rio, Ponto Final (Full Stop), showed the extent to which the Rio state legislature acted in the service of private interests, another core element in the institutionalization of crime. Rio's main bus companies paid bribes to state deputies to block potentially damaging investigations and projects and to approve beneficial legislation. The scheme was basically a *mensalão*, only this time the stipend wasn't paid by the executive but by businessmen under contract with the state.[9] The arrest of top-tier executives from these companies led Calcutta to a figure who had long called the shots in Rio de Janeiro: state deputy and president of the Rio chapter of MDB, Jorge Picciani.

If the Cabral government displayed many of the components of institutionalized crime, the investigations also found most of these clearly demonstrated by the Picciani clan. The patriarch Jorge Picciani was arrested under Operation Cadeia Velha (Old Jailhouse), on charges of brokering the payment of bribes by the state's transport companies to the delegates involved in the scheme. As long-standing Speaker of the State Assembly, Picciani had the power of appointment over key posts within the executive and the prerogative of nominating three titular advisors to the state's auditing body.

True to Brazilian political tradition, two of Jorge's sons followed in their father's footsteps. Leonardo Picciani was elected to Congress and held the post of minister of sports under President Michel Temer. Rafael Picciani was elected to the State Assembly and appointed municipal transport secretary by Mayor Eduardo Paes. The third son did not go into politics but followed his father to jail nonetheless. Felipe Picciani was the son designated with handling the family's private business affairs, especially their fast-growing livestock empire. According to plea-bargain testimony from former state auditor Jonas Lopes, their company, Agrobilara, was used to launder bribe money by falsifying the sale of heads of cattle. According to the charges brought against the Piccianis on March 15, 2018, the clan had a foothold on both sides of the counter, so they could profit from the public and the private sides of the scheme.

The aftermath of Sérgio Cabral's two terms of office as governor of Rio de Janeiro revealed a desolate wasteland: the celebrated Pacifying Police Units (UPPs) set up in the state's slums and shantytowns had proved an utter failure, street crime was rife (over 5,000 murders and 200,000 robberies in 2016 alone),[10] hotels were empty, and the state was broke, with civil-service wages in arrears and suppliers left unpaid.

Just when the state was supposed to be basking in World Cup and Olympic glory, it was plunging to a new nadir, thanks to the disastrous social, political, and economic effects of a criminological phenomenon called "institutionalized delinquency."

A Glimpse of the Whale—a Case in Pernambuco

Jorge Pontes: When I arrived in Recife in February 2007 to take over the FP Superintendency in Pernambuco, I found myself struggling to process something that can only be described as an affront to any self-respecting policeman.

I traveled there from Brasília in the company of two public prosecutors who were to attend my swearing-in at the headquarters of the fifth Regional Federal Court of Pernambuco. No sooner had we left the airport en route to our hotel than I started noticing something strange on practically every corner: a chain of establishments with the same brash neon sign that read "Monte Carlo's." The franchise had stores literally everywhere. When I asked our driver what sort of business it was, he said it was a "chain" that sold bets on the "Jogo do Bicho," a popular but illegal lottery with animals and number sequences.[11]

Not even the largest drug store or fast-food chains had as many premises as Monte Carlo's had in Recife. One of the prosecutors turned to me and joked: "Dr. Pontes, it's an outright insult to the local cops. You'll have to do something about this."

At one of my first meetings with my new team, a few days later, I learned that "Monte Carlo's" was exactly what the driver had said—a chain of illicit but hardly clandestine mini-casinos. However, as illegal gambling is a misdemeanor, and therefore under Civil Police jurisdiction, the "insult" wasn't against the Federal Police as such, but the flagrant disregard for the law rankled us all the same.

In Rio de Janeiro, the guys selling *Bicho* bets sit out on street corners with little wooden crates that can be picked up and moved at the first sign of the police. These are "embarrassment" enough to the authorities, but the situation in Recife was downright offensive, especially because the stores were licensed to operate by city hall. It was a clear case of institutionalized illegality.

Life went on at the superintendency, though we occasionally wondered what we could do to sink Monte Carlo's without treading on the toes of the Civil Police or overstepping our own purview. We needed a concrete reason for targeting the business, one that was indisputably within our remit. One day in April 2007, Police Chief Bernardo Gonçalves de Torres came running into my office saying he had received a tip-off that Carlos Ferreira, the owner of Monte Carlo's, was about to leave São Paulo aboard a private jet with approximately one million reais in cash on his person.

According to the informants, Carlos had gone to São Paulo to buy slot machines for his gambling dens but would be returning with the cash because the deal had fallen through. Chief Bernardo threw a team together and headed for the airport. The plane arrived at Guararapes on time and the racketeer was met by our men out on the runway.

In addition to the cash, of unspecified origin, we seized his laptop. It took just under a week to get a warrant to break into the system, but when we did, Bernardo was able to harvest a treasure trove of damning information—enough to open an investigation into the Monte Carlo's den chain.

In preparing the operation, I took additional care to prevent leaks by entrusting it to the Organized Crime Division. As we were dealing with crimes against the Treasury, it really should have been handled by the Executive Department, which answered to the Treasury Police (CGPFAZ) at the time.

However, I knew that some of the agents with the Executive Department had ties to members of the state government's Social Defense Secretariat, so I thought it best to "interpret" the scheme as falling under "organized crime" and place it in the safe hands of Getúlio Bezerra, an FP icon in the fight against criminal organizations.

On the eve of the operation, I rang the director-general of the Federal Police, Paulo Lacerda, to discuss how things would play out. I told him I was planning on informing the Pernambuco social defense secretary only after our prime target was in custody. Lacerda agreed. He understood that my biggest concern was to avoid the local authorities leaking details of the operation.

Operation Zebra was a complete success. Not long after six in the morning, with Carlos Ferreira under arrest, I rang the social defense secretary to tell him what was happening. I then went up to the audio monitoring sector to follow the phone calls we'd intercepted that morning. As soon as the police showed up, the first thing members of Ferreira's gang did was scamper to ring their lawyers and to tip-off their accomplices. I remember one target who called his lawyer only to discover that the attorney was himself a target of the operation. Mortified, the lawyer struggled for the most euphemistic ways to explain that the police were in his home that very minute. It took a while for the client to catch the drift, but he finally understood that the man he was relying on to spring him from jail would be joining him there forthwith.

The operation dismantled the largest illegal gambling ring outside the Rio–São Paulo axis, and the assets seized included a private jet, a helicopter, two yachts, and twenty luxury automobiles. The federal courts interdicted ten properties belonging to the group and froze approximately fifty million reais in funds.

The investigations revealed that numerous Civil and Military Police officers were involved in the scheme—which justified my move to designate the case to Federal Police departments whose staff had no connections with local authorities. According to the investigators, state cops provided security for the gambling dens and for gang members transporting cash. Ferreira and his mob had evaded somewhere between 135 to 140 million reais in taxes during a five-year period, from the proceeds of their slot machines alone. Twenty federal agents took part in the operation, executing arrest and search warrants across the Greater Recife area, as well as in Rio de Janeiro, Bahia, and São Paulo. Fifteen arrests were made on charges that included money laundering, tax evasion, and contraband.

I had no doubt whatsoever the operation would displease the governor of Pernambuco. If Monte Carlo's operated so flagrantly without any local authority taking action, it was because it was not in the political establishment's interest to put the "chain" out of business.

The news caused quite a stir among the administration of Governor Eduardo Campos.[12] I'll never forget one particular episode: it was early evening and the superintendency was packed with journalists covering Operation Zebra. I was in my office, having a coffee with Police Chief Rogério Galloro, my right-hand man in Recife and future director-general of the FP. Galloro saw things the same way as I did and knew all too well how inconvenient superintendents tended to "fall up." I remember he looked at me with a wry smile and said: "Pontes, after this, don't be surprised if you get appointed head of Interpol."

I knew that operation was going to disgruntle the local powers-that-be. It was one of my first and most intense brushes with the whale of institutionalized crime, in terms of both criminal organizations working within the state apparatus and blowback from the system. About a month after Zebra, I received an invitation that was "too good to refuse": Head of Interpol in Brazil. With that, I left the command of the Pernambuco Superintendency two years ahead of time.

The Police Chief in the Bow Tie

Jorge Pontes: Over the decades, the FP in Brazil's northeastern states has acquired vast experience in repressing the cultivation, transport, and sale of marijuana. Every year, operations are rolled out against these activities, especially in the hinterlands of Bahia and Pernambuco. Federal Police in these states, as in Paraíba and Alagoas, has developed a certain expertise in the crackdown on weed. The operations are usually launched mid-year, when the marijuana plant is ripe for smoking. The closer the operations fall to harvest time, the more efficient they are.

The seizure and incineration of tons upon tons of harvestable *Cannabis sativa* level a heavy blow against this "illegal agrobusiness." As the year's crop goes up in flames, so too does whatever financial return the gangs might have made on their sale of the drug. In the words of Getúlio Bezerra, the FP's line in tackling organized crime is always to "hit the organization with a capitalist approach to criminal activity."

In terms of political influence over the work of the Federal Police, one emblematic case in recent years took place in Bahia in 1993, during the Itamar Franco presidency. The man in charge of the FP at the time was a retired colonel named Wilson Romão, the last person to occupy the post of director-general without having been a Federal Police chief.

The episode in question involved an investigation into a phantom bank account opened in July 1990 at a Citibank agency in Salvador. The chief in charge was Roberto das Chagas Monteiro, an agent from Recife whose probity was beyond all question. Monteiro was an excellent investigator, fluent in various languages, and he had the cultural baggage to match his undeniable competence. He was also known for his trademark bow tie, which he wore at all times.

After only three months in Salvador, Roberto got a break in his investigations: among the cheques paid into this account, he obtained one from TV Bahia, a local station belonging to the all-powerful Antônio Carlos Magalhães, then serving his third term as governor of the state. Monteiro had arrived at this Citibank account through another phantom account, this one with BMC, used by the Bahian businessman Thales Nunes Sarmento, owner of the construction company Sérvia. Among the several key elements Monteiro managed to ascertain about this account—which received a total of $4.8 million in deposits— were that the construction company Odebrecht, a serial offender, also transferred funds into it and that its alleged holders didn't even exist. It so happens the manager of the Citibank account was one Renato Angelo Tourinho, whose brother was a director at TV Bahia. Among those chief Monteiro indicted in the case was an associate of Antônio Carlos Magalhães, Cláudio Chagas Freitas, accused of providing fake duplicates to the police.

It didn't take Roberto long to come to the conclusion that the phantom account was used to ply illicit funds into Antônio Carlos Magalhães' victorious gubernatorial campaign in 1990. So he did the obvious and called Magalhães in for questioning. The governor not only ignored the summons but called the Federal Police HQ in Brasília that night, demanding the director-general's personal phone number. Obviously, the desk sergeant did not give the irate governor of Bahia the director's number, but he did, as per protocol, contact Wilson Romão, who authorized that he do so.

The director-general's home phone rang late that night. On the other end of the line was the Bahian strongman braying that he would have his police "arrest the Federal agent who's up here in Salvador conducting an uncalled-for investigation." It was a clear threat: Wilson Romão was to transfer Monteiro out of Bahia immediately.

The following morning, when Roberto arrived at the superintendency, he received a call from Brasília. It was Nascimento Alves Paulino, the central coordinator of the Federal Police, then second in the chain of command. Nascimento passed on Romão's orders: Monteiro and his assistant were to pack up and catch the first flight back to Brasília, taking all their case files with them. Roberto was at a loss as to what was going on, but Nascimento Paulino was categorical: he was acting on the express orders of the director-general, at the behest of the governor of Bahia, Antônio Carlos Magalhães.

Just as he'd obeyed the order to go to Salvador, he obeyed the order to leave, but Roberto Monteiro was not the type to simply bow to the likes of Antônio Carlos Magalhães, and he took a step that, to this day, serves as an example for younger agents. Seeing how the director-general had buckled under pressure from the Bahia chieftain, he accepted the avocation,[13] but not without first formally registering, in a written dispatch included in the case records, that he had been ordered not only to hand over his case files but to detail all the steps he had taken thus far, and planned to take thereafter, as well as the conclusions he may have drawn from his investigations.

By taking this step, he managed to bind his successor to his discoveries. The director-general tried to lean on him to remove the dispatch from the investigation, but he refused to do so. He said his superiors could do whatever they wished, seeing as the case was no longer under his charge, but he kept a copy of the dispatch and knew full well that no one would dare remove a document from the records. Roberto das Chagas Monteiro's parting shot as head of that investigation had two effects: it spared the Federal Police's blushes, and it gave the public prosecutor's office grounds on which to press ahead with the investigation into those criminal facts. Wilson Romão ended up palming the investigation off to another police chief, who conducted his investigations from a safe distance, in Brasília. There is no record that Governor Antônio Carlos Magalhães was ever heard in connection with the case.

This is an episode—with the 1988 Constitution already in vigor—that warrants remembering, because it shows how our institution needs autonomy. For decades, it was said within the FP that no regional superintendent for Bahia was ever appointed without the approval of Antônio Carlos Magalhães.

Up until the beginning of Paulo Lacerda's tenure in 2003, FP superintendents in the Northeast frequently remained in their posts for years on end. In more recent times, especially in the wake of mega-operations like Lava Jato, the FP has launched several major offensives against crime in the region, rocking the local political elites to their core. Every now and then, young generations of local federal agents come along and shake things up. Today, we're seeing a number of courageous police chiefs who refuse to bend to these chieftains and are totally engaged in tackling institutionalized crime. The career of Pernambuco's Roberto Monteiro serves as a lasting inspiration to these men and women.

Chapter 9

THE OBSTRUCTION OF FEDERAL POLICE INVESTIGATIONS

A single suitcase is perhaps not enough material evidence to determine whether or not a crime has been committed.

Fernando Segovia, former director-general
of the Federal Police

Jorge Pontes and Márcio Anselmo: The secrecy of police operations against criminal organizations embedded within the apparatuses of public power is protected by laws and by legal routines that the police themselves adopt to ensure the inviolability of their work. Secrecy is a universal rule: the fewer people who know, the less chance there is of a leak. Investigations into top-brass government officials can become so complex and delicate that the fear of moles inside the operation can reach paranoiac levels and however extreme that may seem, the justifications are very real indeed.

The procedure starts with the regular day-to-day activities of a chief conducting a police investigation and culminates in tactical operations in the field, such as the execution of search and/or arrest warrants. A major raid can involve hundreds of agents across various cities and states and seldom takes more than five or six hours to complete, unless abundant quantities of cash or jewelry are apprehended or large areas need to be covered. One such case was the raid on the Odebrecht headquarters in São Paulo during the Erga Omnes phase of Car Wash, which began at daybreak and dragged on until 10:00 p.m. that night.

However, for the agents involved, these operations begin hours before dawn. Generally, the teams arrive at the command center at around 3:00 a.m., where they don the now-famous black tactical attire and check the equipment (ranging from flashlights and handcuffs to semiautomatic rifles) before heading to the pre-op briefing—usually held at the local or nearest FP unit. During the operations, there frequently arises the need to request new or supplementary warrants from the magistrate courts—as occurred, for example, on various phases of Car Wash and other mega-operations—so a back-office team has to be in place. The moment we do finally hit the streets is the result of months or even years of proactive investigation, and it's our big chance to gather and analyze material evidence of criminal wrongdoing.

Before going to the magistrate to request warrants, we have to build a solid case, one that will convince the judge that there are strong grounds for probable cause. A lot goes into these affidavits, including discussions with public prosecutors, who advise the judge on whether or not to issue the warrant. The writing of affidavits involves a great deal of in-house debate too, and the chief must also talk to his or her superiors to secure the material and human resources for the ensuing operation. Where these require the allocation of police resources from other FP units or officers with specialist knowledge, such as the ability to speak a certain language, the viability of a mission may need to be analyzed at the administrative level. For example, on the first phase of Car Wash, a certain ring of suspects communicated in Arabic, so an officer with knowledge of the language had to be brought in time and again to translate the intercepted dialogues.

During phase one, there was a curious episode where one of the money-movers under surveillance would switch to French when dealing with sensitive issues. Little did he know that the officer monitoring his dialogues was fluent in the language.

Total secrecy is paramount in cases that stretch out over months and cast a wide net in terms of suspects.

The core investigation of Car Wash, the stem of the sprawling probe we know today, originated from the Banestado case and concerned four money-movers: Alberto Youssef, Nelma Kodama, Raul Srour, and Carlos Habib Chater. The degree of compartmentalization was absurd: those focusing on one *doleiro* knew nothing about the investigations into the others or even of their very existence. The points of intersection among these four lines were the police chiefs Márcio Anselmo—who coordinated the operation and all related judiciary measures—Erika Marena, head of the financial crimes division, and Igor Romário de Paulo, regional chief of the organized crime unit.

It was the best way to ensure that everything went as planned. Insisting on compartmentalization, where information is shared on a need-to-know basis only, was not just motivated by distrust. Sometimes leaks are unintentional, but people can't spill or be weaseled out of details they don't have.

In some cases, attempts to obtain confidential information don't come from higher up the ladder or from inside the Justice Ministry but from people who may have some connection with those working on investigations. When this starts to happen, we know we're onto something big and that the whale is near.

The arrest of former Petrobras director Paulo Roberto Costa, on March 20, 2014, is a clear illustration. The warning bells started to ring early, telling us that Car Wash was digging in the right direction. On the day the director was arrested, an important retired Federal Police chief was seen at the FP Superintendency in Paraná. After retiring from the corporation, Jaber Makul Hanna Saadi, former superintendent of Paraná and São Paulo, had become an associate of the former justice minister Márcio Thomaz Bastos.

His sudden decision to drop in on his former colleagues was taken as a sign that shock waves had been felt. Jaber was probing for information about Car Wash, what it was really about, and who it was targeting. During that same week, Antônio Carlos de Almeida Castro, aka Kakay, one of the most well-connected lawyers in the political world, arrived out of the blue to defend Alberto Youssef. The money-mover had been known to the Car Wash task force for many years, since back during the Banestado investigation, but the fact that Kakay was representing him signaled that some very important people were pulling strings behind the scenes, wanting to know if they were on the radar.

Neither the former superintendent nor the boutique lawyer managed to extract any information that could have jeopardized the investigation, because the agents knew how to protect their work.

The Tensest Day

The day a field op rolls out—D-0, in our jargon—is the tensest of all, and no level of caution is too much. In addition to the chief in charge, the efficiency and dedication of the officers entrusted with coordinating field operations are also key—organization, methods, and logistics are essential elements of success.

There's an infinity of orders, intel, and instructions to share with hundreds of operatives, such as the identity of the targets and whether they are likely to be armed and dangerous, and the size, type, and addresses of the buildings to be searched. There are vehicles, radio equipment, evidence bags, cameras, and cellphones to organize and allot. Crew compositions (clerks, chiefs, forensic team, agents) and roll-out times to decide, target dossiers to distribute, and interview rooms to designate for each suspect brought in. And, depending on the operation, there may be planes or helicopters to scramble, billeting and catering arrangements to be made, and so on.

The night before an op, hundreds of federal agents arrive at the unit that is to serve as base. Some take regular flights, but others fly aboard Air Force Hercules carriers. Those closer to the unit come in unmarked cars. In the mess hall on the eve of an operation, seeing all those black-clad federal agents gathered under one roof gives you a real adrenaline boost. Billeting often happens in local military bases.

Here, once again, everything possible is done to avoid leaks. Just under an hour before roll-out, a final briefing is given at the operational base. Usually it's the area director, from Brasília, who speaks at these meetings, depending on how important the op is considered to be, followed by the regional superintendent, and the chief in charge of the investigation, who provides the team leaders with the questions they are to make during the various interrogations later that day.

The chief in charge, or someone delegated by him or her, will also explain the ins and outs of the scheme under investigation, the suspects involved, and the amount of money syphoned off, and will also give tips and guidance on the kinds of evidence that are most crucial to the case. That done, the agent in charge of structuring and planning the operation will clear up the numerous last-minute doubts that arise. This agent, the operation planner, is the authority who takes care of the logistics (room and board, etc.) and distributes the "mission folders" at the final briefing. These are basically envelopes containing confidential details about each target. All of this is done in the small hours before dawn.

Once again, some phases of Car Wash illustrate the care taken to keep privileged information as watertight as possible. Given the impact and importance of the most successful anticorruption probe in Brazilian history, this sequence of procedures was altered and certain stages dropped. On the most critical ops, for example, the chiefs in charge decided not to brief the few dozen agents taking part, nor did they deliver the traditional "who's who," or draw out any sort of organizational chart. Even the names of the other agents involved were kept from each member ahead of the op.

Agents coming from other states found out who the targets were only at the very last minute. So, rather than post a list of targets on the board, as is usually the case, lists were either not given or the order of the targets was intentionally jumbled (the FP normally lists its targets in order of importance).

There was good reason for taking these extra precautions: figures as powerful as those targeted by Car Wash, people with a lot of money and the nation's leading attorneys on retainer, had the capacity to infiltrate operations.

Under "normal" circumstances, the briefing is followed by questions from the crew, so that any lingering doubts can be clarified. Then it's time to hit the road. Depending on the action, federal criminal forensics teams or forensic auditors from the IRS, audit body, or Treasury may accompany the agents. The crews line up in front of their respective vehicles, where those working together for the first time can make their introductions. This is also where the final checks are made on personal firearms: Glocks, hks, Sig Sauers, Walther ppks.

The vehicles leave in small convoys, in order of distance-to-target, and move fast to ensure the element of surprise.

The crews' arrival and the arrests made are all followed in real time at the Operations Center, and the targets are usually in cuffs within forty minutes of roll-out.

Federal Police operations often happen simultaneously in different cities, so the planning has to be the same for each unit, with corrections for time zone, where necessary. Depending on the reach of each branch of the op, there may be more than one operational coordinator. In other words, the process is decentralized, even if the intelligence never is.

All it takes to ruin all of this is one leak, one mole, but if the operation does go smoothly, there's still a lot of work ahead. Evidence needs to be collected, sorted, and analyzed, and this can take a long time, depending on the volume and type gathered. Not unusually this will lead to new lines of investigation being opened.

This phase has become increasingly important, as greater swiftness in evidence-sorting now triggers successive phases more quickly. On various occasions, the evidence apprehended by one branch of Car Wash spawned an offshoot almost immediately. This occurred with Acarajé and Xepa, and with Pixuleco i and ii, and a third phase would have followed had the case not been transferred to São Paulo.

The various precautions taken to avoid leaks and ensure the efficacy of these dawn raids are indispensable to the overall integrity of our work. But situations do arise, especially concerning the upper echelons of government, when the obstacles posed to an operation go beyond the threat of moles. Sometimes, authorities who are above the Federal Police in the republican hierarchy use their power to steer, block, or even quash certain cases.

There was one such episode that caused enormous repercussion in 1998 and occupies to this day an important place in the annals of national political history.

The Cayman Dossier

Jorge Pontes: It was 2001, and I was coordinating the environmental crimes unit. I was in my office one day when I was called up to see the director-general, Agílio Monteiro, on the ninth floor of the corporation's HO, the so-called Máscara Negra (Black Mask) building in Brasília. It was Wilson Damázio who rang me on my extension. He was second in command at the time and my direct line of report on all things related to environmental crime. We had an excellent rapport, and he was a hardworking boss who knew how to motivate his subordinates. I arrived at the director-general's office to find both men there. Agílio gave me a perfunctory greeting and Damázio, ever direct, got straight to the point:

"Son, an investigation is being opened into facts causing a rumble in the press, and the Presidency is keen to elucidate the alleged crimes."

He told me that, on the spur of a series of stories running daily in the press, the minister of justice was demanding an immediate investigation into certain facts, and he wanted to know what I thought of a fellow chief of police:

"Do you know Paulo de Tarso Teixeira?"

I said that I did. We'd been colleagues since the academy and had always maintained a cordial relationship. Paulo kept his cards close to his chest, but he was a nice guy. We sometimes played soccer together on Thursdays, along with the other staff, Damázio included. I said I would have no problem whatsoever in working with him.

I was sure they were going to give me something extra to do, and I was already going on about how snowed under I was at the Environmental Crimes Division, when Damázio cut me off.

"Pontes, forget about your division for a minute. It's the director-general you're talking to here, son!—he said, raising his voice a little, but without losing his customary professorial and paternal tone."

Put that way, and after hearing from the director-general himself that I was being called upon for my international experience, I agreed to do whatever was necessary and to the best of my ability. I was on my feet and ready to leave when Agílio added that much of the investigative work would be conducted abroad, and that Paulo and I would be given every assistance and resource necessary. The important thing was to get to the bottom of the case in hand.

The investigation, to which I dedicated my time exclusively throughout, came to be known in the press as the Cayman Dossier affair. Though the crime committed is of no direct relevance here, it is important to recall this episode, so widely covered in the press over the last twenty years, because two associated incidents showed me, for the first time in my career, the lengths to which the political elite and occupants of the most important posts in the republic are prepared to go to influence the course of investigations.

In 1998, rumors started circulating in Brasília about some documents that allegedly proved that four leading figures of the powerful PSDB Party—the president himself, Fernando Henrique Cardoso; the governor of São Paulo, Mário Covas; the minister of health, José Serra; and former congressman and party treasurer Sérgio Motta—had millions of dollars tucked away in tax havens in the Caribbean.

When the news broke, the FP started an investigation to prove or disprove the existence and veracity of these documents. Middlemen representing the dossier's authors had ensured a copy of the papers reached Fernando Henrique Cardoso through an anonymous letter addressed to the Presidential Palace. A second copy was sent to José Serra, via fax, at the ministry. Even before the FP opened its investigation, some rather unorthodox decisions began to be made. First of all, Cardoso instructed the presidential guard to start an investigation, something outside its purview and specialization. Hardly surprisingly, the probe didn't get very far.

After that, a further attempt was made through nonofficial channels to discover who was behind the dossier. Former senator Gilberto Miranda was sent to the United States to procure the services of the private risk consulting firm Kroll. Once again, nothing of note was discovered—the final report from Kroll's detectives was inconclusive. Only then did President Cardoso do what he should have done all along: take the case to the Federal Police and public prosecutor's office.

Police Chief Paulo de Tarso was initially put in charge of the case and managed to prove, that same year, that the documents were forgeries. Brazilian businessman living in Miami had bought a company—CH, J&T, opened in Nassau, the Bahamian capital, in 1994—and doctored the records to include documents bearing the forged signature of Sérgio Motta. The idea was to make it look as though he were the owner of the company and that Fernando Henrique, Covas, and Serra were partners in the endeavor. The forgers' plan was to create incriminating evidence that could be sold to PSDB's political opponents here in Brazil and derail Cardoso and Covas' upcoming reelection bids.

Though it was fairly obvious the documents were counterfeit, Paulo de Tarso had not yet managed to identify those responsible. When he sent his report to the Ministry of Justice asking for an extension to the investigation, the attorney general, Luiz Augusto Santos Lima, jumped the gun and indicted three key figures thought to have been involved: former mayor of São Paulo, Paulo Maluf, Mário Covas' main rival in the 1998 gubernatorial election, accused of being one of the buyers; the pastor Caio Fábio dos Santos, accused of brokering the sale; and the former chairman of Banco do Brasil, Lafaiete Coutinho Torres. All three were brought up on libel charges.

Thanks to the AG's precipitousness, the case never did return to Paulo de Tarso and the investigations ended there. There's no way of saying exactly what Luiz Augusto Santos Lima's intentions were in acting the way he did, but he effectively killed the investigation.

The case resurfaced in 2001, when *Globo* newspaper ran an interview, published on March 11, with the US-based Brazilian businessman Oscar de Barros, who had previously been investigated by the US government for crimes against the financial system. He was one of those suspected of having sold the dossier to Brazilian politicians, and he claimed to know who had forged the documents—the "Miami gang," as he called them.[1] As the original investigation had ended without the culprits being identified, and given the repercussion of de Barros' interview, President Cardoso and the minister of justice, José Gregori, ordered the FP back on the case.

That's when I was called in to help Paulo de Tarso, who had led the first investigation. Together, we ended up discovering the identities of the forgers—the businessmen Ney Lemos dos Santos, João Roberto Barusco, Honor Rodrigues da Silva and his wife, Cláudia Rivieri. The group had bought CH, J&T from the American attorney Robert Allen Junior.

Figures from Brazil's political elite were called in for questioning, including Luiz Inácio Lula da Silva, Leonel Brizola, Paulo Maluf, Orestes Quércia, and Fernando Collor, all opponents of PSDB. Also interviewed were Fernando Henrique Cardoso, Mário Covas, and José Serra. Sérgio Motta had passed away in April 1998.

There were some curious incidents during the depositions, which were taken by Police Chief Paulo de Tarso. Concerning former president Lula, we later discovered that he had sent the lawyer Márcio Thomaz Bastos—his future justice minister—to discuss the possible purchase of the dossier. Thomas Bastos flew down south in a private jet, on Lula's request, with the mission of ascertaining the dossier's veracity and the utility of buying it, but he was later discouraged from doing so by Lula himself. Future São Paulo mayor, Marta Suplicy, then still a member of PT, asked to be interviewed in secrecy at her residence. Paulo agreed, but when he left her home after the deposition, he was stunned to find dozens of reporters waiting outside her gate. It's thought that Suplicy, for reasons best known to herself, had tipped off the press.

The first sign that the federal government was not shy about interfering in the investigation came as soon as it was opened. We went to see the then justice minister, José Gregori, who wanted to reinforce the importance of putting the dossier debacle to bed once and for all. As a matter of courtesy, we brought along a copy of the investigation directives, which stated that the case was intended to "elucidate the full circumstances surrounding the Cayman Dossier," as it was called in the press.

When he read the directives, the minister of justice turned to us rather timorously—comically, in hindsight—and asked if we could perhaps elide the words "the full circumstances surrounding."

The impression we were left with was that he wanted us to prove the dossier was false but not to delve too deeply into the matter. I'll never forget it. How removing four words from the directives would have made us investigate less thoroughly is beyond me, but that is what he asked. And though we complied, the minister's request ended up having the opposite to the desired effect. The nitpicking over wording, pathetic though it seemed at face value, sounded to us like a veiled attempt to limit the scope of a Federal Police investigation.

The episode is indicative of how those in high office, and ministers of justice in particular, tend to ignore the need for autonomy in investigations. Gregori's bizarre request was less than republican, but another episode constituted a more concrete, and serious, act of interference in an FP investigation.

While the dossier itself was false, and there was no sign back then of the existence of anything like the institutionalized crime we would see in such a sophisticated form some years later, something the president himself did clearly revealed that politicians have few qualms about trying to manipulate the federal judiciary police force.

Still in 1998, when the dossier was causing a scandal, the owners of CH, J&T tried to take some of the wind out of the investigation's sails. The attorney Emerick Knowles, legal representative of the as-yet-unknown proprietors, was authorized to issue a document, in their name, declaring that Fernando Henrique Cardoso, Mário Covas, and José Serra had absolutely no connection with the company.

The affidavit, a sworn declaration delivered under oath, basically exonerated the trio. But there was one problem: it said nothing about Sérgio Motta, the man whose signature had been forged. Later in our investigations we discovered that the omission of Motta's name had been intentional. As the PSDB campaign treasurer had died in April that year, the criminals figured they could kill two birds with one stone: take some of the pressure off themselves by clearing the other three, while leaving a shadow of doubt over a man who was no longer around to defend himself. After all, they had not, as yet, admitted any forgery had taken place.

A copy of this affidavit reached the Interpol HO in Brasília by fax and was sent from there to the director-general of the FP, Vicente Chelotti. Rather than hand it over to the officer in charge, as he should have, he went straight to the president of the republic.

Chelotti showed the document to Fernando Henrique Cardoso at a house in Brasília, in the company of Supreme Court judge Nelson Jobim and Milton Seligman, former justice minister and the then president of the National Institute for Colonization and Land Reform (Incra). This information was confirmed by the former director-general himself, in federal court, on November 10, 2004.

The document clearing the names of Cardoso, Covas, and Serra was not warmly received by the president of the republic, who took a line of action that was not his to take: he "decided" that the affidavit should not be included in the case files and ordered the director-general of the Federal Police to travel up to the Bahamas to fetch the original.

Chelotti did as he was told. He went to Knowles' office in Nassau and returned with the original affidavit, which he duly delivered to the president. It was never seen again. The Federal Police chief in charge of the investigation never so much as saw it.

It was a clear case of political interference in a Federal Police investigation, witnessed, in fact, by a Supreme Court judge and ordered by the highest office in the land. Cardoso's actions become all the stranger and graver given the fact that he, the president, though a victim of a libelously false dossier, was also, in principle, a person of interest in the case.

The matter would have ended there were it not for the second investigation. The first time Paulo de Tarso and I went to the Bahamas, the lawyer Emerick Knowles agreed to meet us at his office. He pulled out the CH, J&T file and started flicking through it right in front of us. Obviously, he did not give us access to the file, as the real owners of the company—as yet unknown—would certainly have been identified therein. But as he leafed leisurely through the contents, lingering on certain papers, I caught a glimpse of the affidavit and was able to read a snatch of the text. We knew the documents from the first investigation back to front, and I immediately saw that this one was new—to us, at least. The attorney made no attempt to conceal it, so I asked him what it was. He replied, in all tranquility, that it was a copy of an affidavit written at the owners' behest and that he had handed the original over to the Federal Police chief who had come to see him at that very office two years earlier. Paulo de Tarso, trying unsuccessfully to hide his surprise, remarked that it was the first he had heard of that particular document. As the officer in charge of the investigation, it should have been brought to his attention back in 1999.

When we returned to Brazil, we immediately added the missing document to the case file. The newspapers had a field day over the fact that we had found new documental evidence that exonerated the president but incriminated the former director-general, who had buried it. The line taken at the time was that Chelotti had betrayed President Cardoso's confidence by concealing a sworn affidavit that attested to his innocence.

Fernando Henrique Cardoso never commented publicly on the episode, but the appearance of that affidavit was, in fact, material evidence of another crime: the suppression of a public document. In theory, the crime was committed by Vicente Chelotti, who took the fall for it, but there was a partner in crime, and he resided at the Presidential Palace.

We invited Chelotti in for questioning to explain why he had made the document disappear, but he declined and was indicted in absentia. Later, before a court judge, he said that he had gone to the Bahamas to fetch the document on the express orders of the president of the republic and that he delivered it to Cardoso in person as soon as he arrived back in Brazil. He claimed he had no knowledge of what Cardoso had subsequently done with the affidavit. When asked if he had understood the illegality of his actions, he said that he had carried out the order out of "reverential fear"—in other words, as it was a direct order from the commander in chief, he couldn't exactly disobey.

In a deposition given to the Federal Police years later, in 2005, and so after Chelotti's admission before the court, former president Fernando Henrique Cardoso conceded that he had, in fact, ordered the director-general to withhold the document. When asked why, he said that "he reached the decision on the grounds that the contents might have induced interpretations that were politically and economically damaging to the nation." In his deposition, Cardoso also spoke of the moment he received the affidavit:

> He [Chelotti] was pleased with himself, saying that he had successfully demonstrated that we didn't have an offshore account. I said no such demonstration was necessary, because I knew we didn't have one. What I needed to know was who had put the dossier together. That was the point of the matter.

During this period, something happened that just didn't sit right with us, something Paulo and I would only understand a good while later. Right there, I believe, we were sensing the marked cards of Brasília being dealt. The whole situation played out amid a media circus surrounding the ex-director-general, Vicente Chelotti, identified as the sole villain in the story. We'd just returned from Nassau and inserted into the case files the affidavit that had disappeared two years earlier, and which proved the president's innocence in the offshore account case.

Fernando Henrique Cardoso, who had supposedly been betrayed by the head of the Federal Police whom he had appointed to the post, handwrote a letter to the former director-general's father, in which he, to our surprise, heaped praise on Chelotti and declared his unwavering trust in him. It was a letter intended to offer some consolation to an elderly man who was undoubtedly suffering at the sight of his son caught up in such a storm of denigration. It was a gesture, but one that seemed inexplicable to us.

Having worked so hard to prove the president's innocence by bringing home a document that had remained hidden for two years, that public demonstration of support for the former director-general who had suppressed it in the first place was hard to swallow.

After all, it was a tacit negation of our work, and I can still recall how sick it made us feel. It was only two years later, when Chelotti finally got his say in court, that we understood why Fernando Henrique had penned that letter to the disgraced man's father.

For Paulo and I, it was if the ground had fallen out from under our feet. For the presidency, we had done our job too well. By omission, the affidavit, written by Emerick Knowles at the behest of three gougers in Miami, had cast doubt on the name of Sérgio Motta and that was why it was suppressed. Though we would later prove that Motta had no connection to that offshore company either, the damage was done: in acting as it did, the presidency had shown that it had something to fear and wasn't prepared to call anyone's bluff.

Former president Fernando Henrique Cardoso was eventually indicted for his part in the intentional concealment of a public document, but the Federal Court of Brasília saw no grounds on which to pursue the charges against him.

However, the question remained: Why had the president opted to pressure the director-general of the FP into committing a crime rather than simply allowing the affidavit to come to light? Was it because he was afraid that Sérgio Motta, no longer around to clear his name, may actually have been making illegal use of a Caribbean tax haven?

My experience on that investigation, starting with a minister of justice attempting to interfere in the scope of a police investigation, and, later, a director-general of the FP being identified as the culprit in the disappearance of an important document, and on the orders of the president of the republic no less, clearly revealed to me, and perhaps for the first time, that politicians will respect no bounds when it comes to pressuring the Federal Police. It became immediately apparent that there simply had to be a mandate for the post of director-general.

We could finally see what Minister José Gregori had meant when he asked us to edit out the words "full circumstances surrounding," because, by revealing precisely that, we had unearthed events which the government would have preferred to remain dead and buried.

Minister Gregori's less than ethical conduct would cause us further problems over the course of the investigation. While trying to track down the owners of the company and producers of the fake dossier in Miami, we received the help of the FBI, specifically special agent Rick Cavalieros, with whom I already had a rapport. We managed to trace certain figures close to the fraudsters, and we were in the process of piecing together a trail that would lead all the way back to them. We'd identified front companies and even had copies of the cheques used to buy the dossier.

Coincidentally, at around the same time, a Mutual Legal Agreement Treaty (MLAT) was being signed between Brazil and the United States. This agreement conferred greater agility on bilateral cooperation on criminal processes, enabling Brazilian authorities, police chiefs included, to directly request the cooperation of US organs, without needing to go through ambassadorial or diplomatic channels.

In Brazil, the customary channel used was and remains the Department of Asset Recovery and International Legal Cooperation (DRCI), subordinated to the National Justice Department, part of the Ministry of Justice. The MLAT process was far faster and simpler than rogatory letters,[2] for example.

After discovering the criminals' identities and analyzing their modus operandi, we decided to return to Brazil and prepare a lengthy MLAT request. We had not, as yet, approached the suspects in any way, as we wanted to catch them by surprise.

We drafted our MLAT in English and Portuguese, describing the crimes under investigation, the criminal laws infringed, and the articles of law on which we had built our case, as well as the names of everyone we wanted to interrogate and on what grounds. We also asked to subpoena a bank to confirm the clearance of two cheques to the combined total of almost $2 million. The document was forwarded to the authorities in Washington.

We received authorization to travel once again to the United States to interrogate the suspects. When we arrived in Miami, we soon discovered, through one of our witnesses, that a Brazilian journalist was in town and that he had a copy of our MLAT request, including the names of all our targets. I couldn't believe it. All the care we had taken had come to nothing. A few minutes later, we got a call from Brasília saying that a reporter from the weekly magazine *Época* was looking for us in Miami.

So we arranged to meet him. The reporter wanted us to tell him everything in detail, as his report was going to print the following weekend. I asked him not to talk to anyone about anything and to hold off on his report until later, so as not to compromise our investigation. The reporter said he was running his story with or without our input, and that he'd approach our suspects by himself if we chose not to cooperate. This was disastrous, as it would blow the element of surprise.

Over the course of the investigations, after hearing all those involved, we discovered that it was the minister of justice, José Gregori, the authority to whom the DRCI was directly subordinate, who had furnished the journalist with our MLAT request. His reason for doing so was to have something out there as soon as possible that could put to bed any lingering speculation about the president's involvement in the company CH, J&T. And he made sure that happened, even if it meant jeopardizing our investigation.

We'd been betrayed by our own minister. Throughout the investigation, the journalist kept running stories that got in our way, and though the investigation ultimately achieved its objectives, it may well not have, under such adverse circumstances. Sometimes public information is leaked to the press in order to thwart authorities who are attempting to block or hinder investigations, but just as often this kind of leak is done to undercut investigations by making revelations before due process has been carried out. We understand that the press needs scoops and dances to its own tune, but we have to protect the prime objective, which is to clarify crimes and establish guilt. When a leak comes from above, from those who ought to be most zealous of all, it's even more frustrating.

Institutional Leaks

The beginning of the so-called Mega-Operations era came in 2002/4, after Police Chief Paulo Lacerda took over as director-general of the Federal Police during Lula's first term as president. Lacerda rang in some substantial changes in the corporation's methods, aims, and planning, and honed its investigative capacities and actions on the ground. The result was a Federal Police that was staffed and equipped to carry out something as ambitious and complex as Operation Car Wash.

According to FP records, there were only eighteen operations underway in 2003. By 2004, the number had leapt to forty-eight and reached sixty-nine the following year. After that, it was all triple figures, with over 200 operations in course between 2008 and 2013 and over 500 between 2015 and 2016.[3]

Concomitant internal and external factors fueled this new phase at the FP. First of all, hiring began again during the early years of the Lula government, so a young and well-qualified generation of agents came aboard. Investment in technology was also essential to this sharper, abler approach to policing.

As could only be expected, this evolved skillset for fighting corruption, the higher station of those targeted for investigation, and the broader scope of the resulting inquiries spurred an immediate backlash from the system. The political class was rattled, so the pressure we experienced on the job rose considerably and would continue to do so for the next fifteen years. Directors and superintendents started being probed about their operations, surreptitiously at first but then more blatantly and aggressively.

Generally speaking, the FP has consistently shown itself to be resistant to this kind of coercion, and it is a source of pride for us to belong to an institution whose members are not easily corrupted. The corporation's recent string of successes largely comes down to the way most chiefs and agents stand firm against political strong-arming and ensure the confidentiality of the information under their care.

One way the system has found to get around this is to "institutionalize" leaks—a practice that has become disturbingly frequent in recent years. Sometimes it is done subtly, but occasionally no effort at all is made to hide it.

A classic case of an attempt at institutionalized percolation came on March 2, 2012, during the first Dilma Rousseff administration. The president and her minister of planning, Miriam Belchior, signed Decree 7,689, designed to set "limits and levels of governance for the procurement of goods and services and for expenditure on room, board and travel."

Among a series of changes and directives, the Trojan horse being sent to the FP lay in Article 7:

> Only Ministers of State and the directors of organs directly subordinate to the President of the Republic can authorize expenditure on room-and-board and air fares in cases referring to:
>
> i. Redeployments of civil servants or military personnel for unbroken periods exceeding ten days;
> ii. Forty or more days of redeployment in the field, in total, per servant, per year;
> iii. Relocation of ten people or more to the same event; and
> iv. Travel abroad.

In particular, item (iii) was a disaster for FP operations. In our case, it meant that any time we sent ten agents or more to conduct an operation, as is usually the case on major investigations, we had to get express authorization from the minister of justice. This was tantamount to giving the minister and the government a heads-up as to where and when an operation was going to take place. At the time, the minister of justice was PT stalwart José Eduardo Cardozo.

With only 123 units serving the nation's 5,500 or so municipalities, almost all of our large-scale operations required travel-and-board authorization from the minister under these terms. Item ii was another damaging aspect of the decree, as agents working on major intelligence-gathering operations almost always spend more than forty days per year traveling. The upshot was this: what looked, at first glance, to be a purse-tightening decree was actually a way the government could institutionalize a drip line of sensitive information and stay two steps ahead of our investigations.

Certain phases of large and even medium-sized operations require fifty, sixty, or up to a hundred agents. Having to request prior authorization from the government meant targets inside the system would almost certainly be tipped off. The reader will hardly need reminding that most of those under investigation by Car Wash, for example, were either part of the government or very closely connected to it.

During Car Wash, it was essential to keep information as compartmentalized as possible, even within the task force itself. Our investigations were based in Paraná, but most of our targets were in São Paulo, Rio de Janeiro, and Brasília, so the decree made it impossible for us to request operation-level relocations or resources in any of those cities without triggering alarm bells. One way or another, at least the decree didn't expect us to identify the case or targets in question, which would have been absurd even by that government's standards. Clamor from society and public opinion were very important in ensuring the continuation of our work and preventing the government from tying the FP's hands altogether by refusing to allocate the required resources. This norm remained in vigor until the short-lived tenure of Eugênio Aragão as minister of justice, in 2016, during Dilma's second term of office.

During her reelection campaign in 2014, Dilma boasted often and loudly about the operations the FP had carried out during her administration. It was electoral opportunism far from grounded in the facts. Whenever possible, the Dilma government did what it could to throw obstacles in our path.

Dilma's Phantom E-Mail

It was with the onset of the mega-operations in 2003 that the political pressure—and pressure from political appointees—became stronger. Experienced agents who have reached positions of command know how to identify such movements. For example, when a governor chooses a Federal Police chief as his or her Secretary of Security, it often signals an attempt to garner proximity to the FP's regional superintendent. That's not necessarily harmful, but it can be driven by less than republican motivations.

In this context, it is essential that those responsible for investigations ensure the maximum possible level of operational confidentiality. Obviously, this is done within the bounds of the law, and all operations are conducted with judicial authorization, with the investigators reporting on those cases to their immediate superiors—almost always the regional superintendent.

As such, in theory, not even the director-general needs to be in the loop, especially when it comes to the identity of the targets of an investigation. At the very most, the superintendent and his deputies encumbered with the logistics should only know enough about an operation to be able to authorize the human and material resources it requires. Naturally, if the head of the FP doesn't need to know, the minister of justice certainly doesn't.

Of course, it's not always possible to keep things watertight, and at least one significant leak happened at a crucial moment of Operation Car Wash. In their plea-bargain depositions, the marketeers João Santana and Mônica Moura[4] mentioned that they had been tipped off about their arrest by no one less than the president of the republic, Dilma Rousseff, who had been informed of the move by the justice minister, José Eduardo Cardozo.

In February 2016, the couple was in the Dominican Republic, where they were working on the local presidential campaign. Operation Acarajé, under which the pair were to be taken into custody, was scheduled for the 22nd of that month. According to Mônica Moura, on the 20th or 22nd, then president Dilma got in contact asking to speak to João Santana on a "secure line." Moura and Dilma had a special method for secure communication: they used the drafts folder of an e-mail account to which they both had access. When they needed to talk, they would drop draft e-mails into this folder and the other would respond by simply editing the draft.

The couple were supposed to be returning to Brazil through Panama on February 22, the day chosen for the operation. In his plea-bargain testimony, João Santana confirmed that he postponed this return after being informed of his imminent arrest. The couple's lawyers convinced them not to flee and to fly back to Brazil the following day. Even though Santana never acknowledged that he knew he would be taken into custody upon arrival, the fact that they traveled with no cellphones or laptops suggests the opposite. Cardozo denied leaking the information to the marketeers, but the really serious implication of all this isn't the leak itself, but just how fragile it reveals the whole process to be.

It's no surprise that a minister with various fellow party members in the firing line should attempt to interfere in, or at least obtain confidential information about, the ongoing investigations. Of the five police chiefs interviewed for the director-general's post by the newly sworn-in minister, three mentioned to close associates that one of Cardozo's prime concerns was how and when he would be informed of the corporation's operations. At the time, the FP had already been going after white-collar criminals in the upper echelons of government for at least seven years.

The minister of justice's unhealthy curiosity about FP activities is a major problem during these times of institutionalized crime. The minister is the president's right-hand man on all matters relating to the police and is an open channel for all sorts of pressure from the political and business milieus to quash this or that investigation.

One Hundred and Eleven Days of Mixed Signals

In November 2017, President Michel Temer, the vice-president who supplanted the impeached Dilma Rousseff, decided to replace then director-general Leandro Daiello, the longest-standing head in the FP's history. The chosen substitute was Fernando Segovia. As the president was himself under investigation in a number of ongoing cases—as well as other accusations bogged down at Congress—the selection process drew particular scrutiny.

For the press, Segovia had been chosen to try to protect the president and his closest allies, and various details were brought to light to support that thesis. On November 9, the *Folha de S.Paulo* columnist Bernardo Mello Franco wrote that "minister Eliseu Padilha had been lobbying for Segovia" and that "his sponsors for the post included notorious figures from the president's party, PMDB," as well as Augusto Nardes, at the auditors' court. The day before, on November 8, 2017, *Globo*'s Andreia Sadi wrote in the G1 news portal that "[Former president and Maranhão strongman] Sarney had lobbied for the new director-general at a meeting with Temer." José Sarney was Brazil's first post-dictatorship president and had long ruled the notoriously corrupt state of Maranhão as his personal fiefdom. Segovia had occupied the post of superintendent there.

During the 111 days Segovia occupied the post of director-general of the FP, he issued internal and external signals that the press had been right and that he was intent on working to at least obtain more control over the investigations into the activities of his political *compadrios*.

During the press conference held to present him as the new director-general, Segovia delivered a statement that would go straight into the annals of Brazilian politics. He came out with the incredible contention that "a single suitcase" full of money is perhaps not enough material evidence to determine whether or not a crime has been committed.

Segovia was referring to the former congressman Rodrigo da Rocha Loures (PMDB), who was filmed leaving a pizzeria in São Paulo carrying half a million reais in cash in a suitcase. The video surveillance of Rocha Loures was part of what we call a controlled action, a strategy, provided for under the Organized Crime Law, that involves delaying the denouement of an operation (i.e., the apprehension of the suitcase and arrest of Rocha Loures) in order to see what further evidence can be obtained by allowing the situation to take its course. In this case, it proved extremely successful. On the night in question, the former congressman was followed to a pizzeria in the affluent Jardins neighborhood of São Paulo, where he was caught on camera receiving the mystery suitcase. According to the public prosecutor's office, the cash in that travel bag was bribe money from the animal protein giant JBS, and it was destined for President Michel Temer, who had appointed Loures his contact with the company.

Days later, Segovia trotted out a series of declarations that exposed his subordinates and that effectively put in check the activity of the FP. Reiterating his criticisms of the Rocha Loures operation in the popular weekly magazine *Veja*, he promised to "make the Federal Police more republican." And when asked if it was not already republican, he remarked: "It is, but with some inconsistencies. Every now and then we see it overstep its purview and act in a politically biased manner."

Saying that the corporation under his charge was acting with political bias was a bungling attempt to expound a critical vision of the force, and by generalizing the way he did, the director-general put us all in the same basket. However, when asked to get down to the brass tacks of specific cases, Segovia kept tripping over his own feet, especially because his criticisms were, in our view, completely unfair to start with. A case in point was the Operation Carne Fraca (Weak Flesh), which had a negative impact on the country's exports. For the new director, the operation, which exposed corruption schemes within the Ministry of Agriculture, "was just ham-fisted marketing by the Federal Police."

In the same interview, the new head of the FP railed against subordinates who were already receiving heavy criticism in the press.

One of these was Police Chief Erika Marena, who'd been under fire for her work on fraudulent disbursements to the Federal University of Santa Catarina, an investigation that led to the rector's suicide. She bore the brunt of Segovia's public thrashings, but he also singled out Operation Car Wash, already recognized, by that time, as one of the largest corruption probes in history.

The chiefs in charge of the Supreme Court's Investigations Group (Ginq), specially created to conduct investigations ordered by the STF, were also taken aback by some minor changes ushered in by Segovia.

Investigations targeting senators, members of Congress, and other politicians usually require special precautions when these figures are brought in for questioning, and it had been no different under Leandro Daiello, Segovia's predecessor. Whenever a political heavyweight needed to be heard, he or she was allowed to park in the underground garage at the Federal Police HQ and wait in the director-general's anteroom. It was protocol, out of respect for the office held, and they were even served coffee before their depositions.

Segovia took this deference further when it came to investigations involving the president, Michel Temer. Police Chief Cleyber Lopes, a member of the Supreme Court Investigations Group, was the lead investigator on the Ports case, a cash-for-decree probe in which Michel Temer was suspected of receiving bribes in return for the passing of a decree that changed port-area regulations to the benefit of the companies working in the sector (the corruptors in the case).

Lopes was another of Segovia's targets of choice in an incendiary interview given to the news agency Reuters on February 9, 2018. Segovia claimed that there was no evidence whatsoever of any criminal wrongdoing on the part of the president, the prime suspect:

> Well, the grounds for suspicion are extremely fragile, in fact, as to whether any undue influence was exercised, because, in theory, the decree was not issued to benefit that particular company.
>
> Indeed, what we are seeing is that the decree did not, in fact, benefit that company at all. In theory, if there was corruption, or any act of corruption, there is no identifiable beneficiary of that illicit act. No such benefit was obtained. And there is no mention, no trace, as yet, of the money allegedly paid.

One of the conditions we value most highly—indeed, one of the fundamental reasons for having a police force that serves the state, not the governments that run it—is the autonomy of the lead investigator on any case. When the director-general comes out and publicly recommends the course an investigation should take, it amounts to immense and untoward pressure in detriment of that autonomy.

Things got even worse further on in the Reuters interview. Segovia suggested that Cleyber Lopes might end up facing disciplinary proceedings over the way he had conducted the investigation, especially the series of questions he had sent, in writing, to President Michel Temer, who had apparently objected to the tone adopted. In one of his replies, Temer wrote: "I respectfully highlight the impertinence of the question, insofar as it assails my honor and personal dignity."[5]

Segovia's interview sounded like a threat, and Cleyber understood it as such. He also considered it a warning to other chiefs investigating the president's long-term allies. There were, at the time, ongoing cases involving most of the president's men: Henrique Eduardo Alves, Eliseu Padilha, Geddel Vieira Lima, and Eduardo Cunha, to name just a few. If they all felt similarly "offended," they could follow the director-general's suggestion and call for disciplinary action against their investigators.

Segovia's public attack on a subordinate heightened the tension surrounding the Ports inquiry. In the halls of the Federal Police HQ, some were predicting a silent David-versus-Goliath duel between an investigator and the director-general. At a meeting with Eugênio Ricas, the director of the Organized Crime Department, and in the presence of the entire Supreme Court Investigations Group, Cleyber voiced his concern about Segovia's behavior, quoting, to that end, the fateful interview in which he had claimed that half a million in cash in a suitcase was not, in itself, proof of a crime. In addition, equally worrying were the accounts in the press of unscheduled and undocumented meetings between Segovia and Temer at the Presidential Palace—meetings that appeared in neither man's official agenda.

On two occasions, a surreptitious tête-à-tête of this kind came just before the president's palatial depositions on the Ports bribery probe. One of these meetings occurred only days before Gustavo do Vale Rocha, subsecretary for Legal Issues at the Chief of Staff's office and the president's closest legal advisor, was due to be heard by the investigators. During an intercepted phone call between Rocha and Rocha Loures, Temer's middleman with the port-area companies, the legal aide was heard voicing his concern over "the major exposure" the president risked by issuing a decree that tinkered with port legislation. On the occasion, when confronted with his extra-official visit to the Presidential Palace, Segovia said he had visited Temer to discuss "border policing."

Another off-the-agenda visit came the very week Temer was to reply in writing to Cleyber Lopes' fifty questions on the Ports case. On Monday, January 15, 2018, Temer received Segovia at the palace. This time, the explanation the director-general gave journalists for his unscheduled visit was the need "to discuss public security."

In response to the threat against Cleyber, the Supreme Court Investigations Group wrote an official memorandum to the director of the organized crime unit affirming that they would "not endure, whether on case 4621/STF or any other investigation under the entity's care, threats of whatever kind against the technical and functional autonomy of the group's members, or any act that might endanger the party-political neutrality of its operations."

In addition to this swift response from the investigators themselves, there was a severe backlash from associations representing Federal Police chiefs, as well as from the press and from society as a whole. The director-general tried to beat a retreat and issued a mea culpa, saying that he had been misinterpreted and had never intended to interfere in the investigations in any way. Supreme Court judge Luís Roberto Barroso, the authority in charge of the Ports case, demanded clarification from the director-general and ordered that he make no further public pronouncements on the investigation.

Cleyber resisted the pressure and completed his work in October 2018, indicting President Michel Temer for passive corruption and money laundering. Charges were also brought against ten other people, including Temer's daughter, Maristela, whose seven-figure home renovations had been paid for with bribe money from port-area companies.[6]

The year 2018 ended with the public prosecutor's office sending its criminal case against Temer and co. to the Supreme Court.

Attempts by the director-general to intimidate a police chief have gone down in the history of the Federal Police, underscoring more than ever the importance of shielding the FP from political interference.

The episode made it crystal clear that the director-general appointed only months earlier by the president of the republic was working against the corporation, weakening it from within. What nobody knew at the time was that, on February 9, 2018, what the corporation's head was really trying to do was spring an "institutional leak," one of the ways the corrupt political system uses to stifle attacks against the capos of white-collar crime.

Chapter 10

POLITICAL APPOINTMENTS

In fact, what we have seen installed in this country in recent years, as revealed now by Car Wash, is a corrupt model of governance. Something that deserves to be called by its true name, kleptocracy.

Supreme Court judge Gilmar Mendes, in 2015

Jorge Pontes and Márcio Anselmo: On the afternoon of February 9, 2018, the director-general's office sent out an e-mail to the recruitment departments of all twenty-seven regional superintendencies under the title "Recruitment. Provision of the Police Investigation Number."

It read:

Dear Regional Superintendents and Recruitment Heads,

First of all, my compliments to all. In light of the new standardization of the recruitment sector and in function of the pilot tests of the "sismob" system within the FP personnel management department; I hereby:

Instruct those responsible for recruitment to include the *number of the police investigation* in field 9—"mission/service description" on the standard requisition form whenever personnel is being recruited from other states for the launch of an operation.[1]

If it weren't for certain key details, this would have been just one more bureaucratic memorandum fired off to the regional superintendents, outlining yet more procedural instructions. In fact, to those not familiar with FP mechanisms, the message looks harmless enough.

But having to supply the case number on a requisition form basically means relinquishing all control over confidentiality, and in the Brazil of today, with so many top-brass authorities in the investigative crosshairs, the demand struck us all as beyond absurd. Once again, it filled everyone at the FP with the suspicion that the director-general was working against the institution's autonomy.

The work of the Judiciary Police is—and needs to be—eminently technical, protected from all species of political oversight or interference. The police investigates the truth of the facts, and the only individuals who ought to have access to the details of an investigation are those working directly on the case in hand, that is, judges, public prosecutors, forensic teams, agents, clerks, and police chiefs. Absolutely nobody else.

It was bad enough that we now had to seek the justice minister's approval for the redeployment of agents from other states, as per Dilma Rousseff's decree of 2012, but forcing us to provide the investigation number was totally unacceptable—it was tantamount to making us give up the gold, show all our cards. Exposing the investigatory process in this manner risked jeopardizing the outcomes of months of painstaking work.

Besides going against everything that had always been standard practice at the Federal Police, there was no reasonable justification for this invasive measure. The argument given was that it was a question of management and that the director-general, as the occupant of a "position of trust," needed to know what was going on down the ranks. The question was: Whose trust? The fact that the FP's highest officer is appointed by the president of the republic provides the answer. The preservation of the corporation's independence and the autonomy of the lead investigator on a case are bedrock principles of the institution, and they have to stay that way, but under Temer's appointee Fernando Segovia, they were being seriously undermined.

This episode further tarnished Segovia's image before his subordinates and made his position untenable. He was fired from the director-general's post at the end of February 2018.

The "Cleaning Crews" and "Rescue Teams"

The executive has the prerogative of appointing key personnel to the organs that will inspect, audit, regulate, and rule on all matters pertaining to its activities. The justices who sit on the Supreme (STF), superior (STJ), and audit courts (TCU) hold ministerial positions and are appointed by the executive. At state level, the tribunals and auditors' bodies are all collegiate organs stocked wholly or in part by political appointees.

The fact that the executive wields the pen that appoints key figures in the legislature and judiciary is deleterious to the independence and autonomy of these oversight and judicial organs. An attempt to "correct" this problem was to give higher-court appointees life tenure. The idea was to prevent presidents sacking and replacing justices, and thus ensure that they had more freedom to rule as their consciences dictated, without worrying about incurring the wrath of the powerful. It was the kind of amendment that not only failed to correct the original defect but heaped a new one on top of the old: more often than not, job security does little to erase the debt of gratitude and bond of patronage.

The basic result of all this is that the political oligarchies try to secure dual protection in matters judicial: first of all, they appoint their people to the auditing court (a consultative body with no judicial power), so that their accounts can be given a clean bill of health. These are the "cleaning crew," who gloss over or turn a blind eye to the irregularities in public works contracts, tenders, and other governmental expenditures. As such, accounts that don't add up, tenders rigged to favor cartels, and flourishes of creative accounting all get approved in order to please the more influential governors, even in the face of qualified or adverse opinions.

On the judicial level, the Supreme and superior courts, which hear cases against elected officials, often serve as a safe haven for those who wield enough influence. As they have the last word on criminal rulings, they have the power to overturn preventive detentions, postpone sentences pending further rounds of appeal, and interpret the jurisprudence and constitution as they see fit, often frustrating the results of criminal prosecutions across the land. In this sense, they are the "rescue team," the *politico*'s "get-out-of-jail-free card."

The result is our incarceration paradox: on one hand, the jails are woefully overpopulated with the poor and underprivileged, who can't afford lawyers able to exploit the countless loopholes in Brazilian legislation or gain access to the judge's chambers, where they can get a continuance or have trials dismissed. On the other, there is notorious impunity among the rich and powerful, for whom conviction and sentencing are no guarantee they will actually see the inside of a jail.

If the political appointment of higher-court and auditors' court justices is damaging to democracy and paves the way for institutionalized crime to equip itself with "cleaning crews and rescue teams," we have to take care to ensure that the choice of director-general of the Federal Police does not become another form of control, a sort of gardener-in-chief, snipping investigations in the bud.

Over the last fifteen years, with the police bearing down on criminal organizations within the government, the minister of justice has become a key portfolio for the executive and one everyone vies to fill. But today, it is far harder to put forward a name for the director-general's position than it is for the ministry itself.

The FP needs to be an organ of the state but never of the government. As the director-general has the duty to resist political pressure, she cannot consider herself a member of the government that appointed her, even if that autonomy ultimately costs her the job. Recently, anxious to replace the standing director-general, a minister of justice made it a precondition that the new incumbent replace all twenty-seven regional superintendents, with the clear objective of ousting the superintendent for Paraná, home of Operation Car Wash.

All too often, the bolder, more independent agents are overlooked for promotions and appointments within the Federal Police. On this point too, extreme vigilance and social pressure will be needed to prevent the government from transforming the Justice Ministry and directorship of the Federal Police into expedient means of stifling investigations or leaking vital information, as we have seen happen time and again.

Lastly, it would be ideal if the executive could be stripped of the prerogative of appointing the director-general altogether, but that would require a change in the prevailing legislation. The way the Brazilian state has been overrun with crime, the ability to choose an attorney general or director-general of the FP has become, in the final analysis, the chance to handpick your own opponent, the adversary you will meet across the institutional table.

The King's Fifth

Besides the investigatory and judicial organs, the auditing and inspection bureaus also constitute a frontier where political appointments are key to weaving a protection network around institutionalized crime. State audit courts (TCEs, *tribunais de contas estaduais*), encumbered with reviewing the financial statements of the 27 state governments and over 5,500 municipal administrations nationwide, are a perfect example of how the appointment of yes-men can pervert the role these bodies ought to perform—otherwise put, auditors are appointed precisely *not* to improve the quality of public administration.

In general, the TCEs are made up of career auditors who produce technical reports and conduct serious audits. They scrutinize accounts to track and trace exactly how public money is being spent, and they generally do it competently and honestly. The problem is that the audit advisors—the "judges" appointed to the audit courts, those who will vote on whether or not to approve the accounts rendered by the governors—are political appointees. When the technical team conducts an audit on a public works project, or the annual budget versus expenditure, they will often flag irregularities that should, in theory, lead to sanctions, but which are frequently ignored by the advisors put there for precisely that purpose by the governor or mayor. The rules for the composition of the TCE vary from state to state. Thanks to the Car Wash task force, the audit body in Rio de Janeiro became a vital case study.

The Rio State Constitution establishes that the seven members who sit on the audit court be chosen as follows: four are appointed by the Legislative Assembly and three by the governor. Of these three, one is "wholly discretionary," one must be a member of the Public Auditors Body, and the third has to be drawn from a pool of TCE reserve advisors.

This structure allows the legislature and the executive to share the selection of the "cleaning crew." As is common in Brazilian politics, the mayors of today were yesterday's state assemblymen, so those with executive ambitions will want to have their say in who the legislature should send to the audit court. As the appointment comes with life tenure, getting one of your own appointed to the court means you'll have a friendly face there when the time comes.

Operation Quinto do Ouro (The King's Fifth)[2] shed light on the various modalities of collusion that this type of relationship can generate. In addition to ample evidence obtained by the Federal Police and Public Prosecutors' Office in Rio de Janeiro, the King's Fifth was largely based on the plea-bargain testimony provided by Jonas Lopes, former president of the Rio Audit Court. Lopes' testimony led to the detention of the then Speaker of the State Assembly, Jorge Picciani, who, as we have seen, would end up facing corruption charges under later phases of Car Wash, specifically for receiving bribes from businessmen with contracts with the state government.

On this occasion, however, Picciani was suspected not of receiving bribes but of organizing the payment of bribes to TCE advisors, some of whom he had been instrumental in having appointed to the post in the first place. Jonas Lopes confirmed to the investigators that he and his colleagues had been receiving monthly payments of at least 100,000 reais each for years in order to turn a blind eye to irregularities in Rio government contracts and to approve the municipal and state accounts.

On the main public construction projects conducted by the government of Sérgio Cabral, the deal with the companies that made up the cartels was that a percentage skimmed off the total would go to the judges on the state's audit court. In other words, the contracts were padded from the outset to pay the executive, for granting the contracts, and the TCE, for overlooking their irregularities and for lending airs of legitimacy to the fraudulent system.

According to the depositions and evidence gathered, this was the case on the billion-real overhaul of Maracanã Stadium[3] and on the construction of the Metropolitan Ring Road. In one piece of incontrovertible evidence obtained by the investigation, the former president of the TCE-Rio, Aloysio Neves, was caught on tape telling transport-sector businessman Marcos Andrade Barbosa Silva all about the monthly sweetener and the one million reais bribe he had received on the Maracanã concession.[4]

And that wasn't all. In addition to the cut separated for the audit court, the advisors also abused their positions on a "retail" basis, something that certainly occurs Brazil-wide. For example, an audit court judge reviewing the accounts of a hinterland mayor may negotiate a bribe directly with that figure in return for a clean bill of financial health. There is a term the advisors use among themselves when referring to these noncollegiate arrangements: "flying solo."[5]

Operation Quinto do Ouro led to the arrest of five members of Rio's TCE in 2017. Counting Jonas Lopes, who turned state's witness, six out of the seven members of the audit court were implicated in the scheme and were stripped of their life tenure and posts.

The only member of the TCE not accused of any wrongdoing was Marianna Montebello, and there is a good reason for that. Montebello was the advisor drawn from the Public Audit Body, in other words, she was the only one who was not a political appointee. When the scandal broke, she became interim president of the court, and the vacant chairs were filled from the pool of substitute advisors, all of whom were career auditors.

The result of this radical, if forced, change of profile was no surprise. Just a few months after being restocked, the TCE in Rio was taking a far more technical and rigorous line in its reviews. In 2018, the newspaper *O Globo* reported on this comparative spike in productivity. By April 22 of that year, the 2016 accounts for sixty-nine of the ninety-one municipalities under its jurisdiction had been reviewed and fifty-one of those rejected. The contrast with earlier years could not have been starker. When the court was still staffed by executive and legislature appointees the number of accounts rejected was far lower: just eight out of ninety-one in 2015, three in 2014, and one in 2013. In 2012, the closing year of municipal administrations, when rejections tend to be higher, twenty-six were denied endorsement.

The new audit court also rejected the state government's accounts for the year 2016. It was the first time this had happened since 2002. In other words, all the accounts submitted to the TCE by the notoriously corrupt Sérgio Cabral administration (2007–14) had been passed, despite the dozens of corruption scandals affecting almost every department.

The *O Globo* report flagged another revealing comparison too: the new composition of the audit court had also ruled to cancel the results of sixty-six public tenders on the grounds of irregularities. Together, these sixty-six contracts totaled four billion in state funds. The previous year, under the old composition, the total in suspended tenders was 1.8 billion reais—an increase of 122 percent from one year to the next.

The Rio case is a particularly damaging example of what happens when corruption is institutionalized down to the audit court. It is certainly not the only one, but it does serve as a warning for how such organs can be co-opted by institutionalized crime and used to cover its tracks and lend a gloss of probity to the most corrupt administrations.

Chapter 11

THE CURRENT ROLE OF THE FEDERAL POLICE

The Constitution and the rule of law are not partisan political tools. Lady Justice wears a blindfold. She is not supposed to peek out to see how her political master wishes her to weigh a matter.[1]

James Comey, former director of the FBI

Jorge Pontes and Márcio Anselmo: When cadets join the Federal Police Academy, they hear time and again, from countless police chiefs teaching there, that we are the Brazilian FBI. That's not entirely an exaggeration. When the Federal Police Department was modernized in the late 1960s, it was recast in precisely that mold. The former Federal Public Security Department (DFSP) was a mix of the Guanabara Civil Police—a throwback to when Rio was still the national capital—the Military Police, and the Special Guard in Brasília. It was this lack of an identity of its own that inspired the need to create a new, more agile force to reflect the aspirations of the modern, purpose-built new capital, Brasília.

It was then that a group of new inspectors (as police chiefs were called at the time), fresh out of the 1969 academy class, took the idea for a new Federal Police to then director of the DFSP, General Nilo Caneppa. Some of this group, which included Nelson Marabuto, João Batista Campelo, Fernando Santana, Hélio Romão, and Raimundo Mariz, had been part of a mission sent to benchmark the British and German police forces and the American FBI. After their return, the general consensus was that the Federal Bureau of Investigation would be the best model to follow.

Police Chief José Roberto Benedito Pereira, former inspector-general and ex-director of the National Police Academy, was a member of the class of 1972, the first haul of graduates from the newly minted FP, the so-called new blood. According to José, many members of the benchmarking mission were instructors on that course, and almost all the class materials used were American. The main idea was to instill new concepts about policing, many of them imported from the FBI, and the focus was on restructuring the intelligence aspects of the job.

This infusion of "new blood" was a watershed in the history of Brazil's FP, as was the crop of new police chiefs who emerged from the academy between 1995 and 2003. Sometimes, the FP's ranks are joined by an influx of new recruits from the educated middle class, who go on to overhaul the corporation, bringing renewal and growth. Countless prominent agents and chiefs who made decisive contributions to the development of policing in Brazil came from these "golden" classes.

When the FP was restructured, Brazil was still under military dictatorship, and it was a time when the armed forces put repression and investigation first. During that period, and even more so post-redemocratization, the FP took on a host of attributions that, in the United States, for example, are the remits of separate organs: the DEA handles drug-related crime, the Secret Service is responsible for protecting the nation's authorities and investigating counterfeiting, the Bureau of Alcohol, Tobacco, Firearms and Explosives (ATF) deals with all weapons-related offenses, the Department of Homeland Security looks after immigration services, and the Fish and Wildlife Service investigates crimes relating to fauna and flora.

The Brazilian Federal Police is responsible for all those areas *and* the expedition of passports and immigration control, the regulation and inspection of private security firms, the investigation of crimes against indigenous communities, crimes against the financial markets, and others. The fact is, the FP handles more fronts alone than all the American federal agencies together.

Being able to accompany the activities of the FBI is an invaluable experience for any Brazilian police officer. Beyond the working conditions provided, and the technology and equipment they have at their disposal, the legal protection the FBI enjoys is something our country can only aspire to achieve someday. The autonomy the FBI is assured is truly impressive in comparison with what we've got here in Brazil. There, no American congressman or senator would dare suggest cutting the FBI budget or making legal changes that might restrict or obstruct its functioning. Anyone who tried would instantly come under suspicion for attempting to sabotage the state's capacity to tackle crime.

Another healthy characteristic of the FBI that should be applied here is the fact that the bureau does not lease out its agents to any other organs, whether federal, state, or municipal. The Brazilian FP, on the other hand, loans out its agents, scientists, and police chiefs on all sorts of duties, even as aides to senators and members of Congress. The FBI does nothing of the sort.

In Washington, there's the Office of Congressional Affairs (OCA), a unit that functions as a liaison between the FBI and Congress. The FBI agents who work at this office inform Congress on a range of issues and assist with congressional hearings, but OCA agents remain, over and beyond all else, bureau personnel.

Another major difference between the Brazilian Federal Police and American FBI concerns its relationship with other police forces. Unlike FP agents, American feds are never posted to local police departments, like the NYPD or LAPD, but their assistance would hardly be needed there anyway, as these are extremely well-equipped corporations. The Brazilian Federal Police needs to evolve on numerous fronts, especially in terms of working conditions and legal protections, but the reality of Brazilian policing is far more precarious than in the United States. In recent years, Brazil has seen its Civil Police Force—the nation's investigative police—fall into disarray, underfunded, undertrained, and under-equipped. In the major urban centers, the Military Police, responsible for repressive policing, has been swept up in an uncontrollable tsunami of violence.

The Last Target of Operation Car Wash: The Judiciary

If Car Wash broke new ground in picking apart the corruption at the Rio de Janeiro Court of Auditors, there is one branch of the apparatus that, in general terms, remains untouched by the investigation: the judiciary. At the executive, the fight against corruption reached the top of the pyramid, putting governors and even a former president of the republic behind bars. At the legislature, senators and congressmen previously considered "untouchable" have been taken down, and in the private sector, captains of industry and powerful tycoons have ended up doing hard time.

But five years into the corruption probe, the judiciary remains unscathed. Threats to "give up" the nation's leading gavel-wielders have not escalated beyond bluff-calling or message-sending that, in the final analysis, amounted to nothing but "cries for help." It would be naive to imagine that the dearth of indictments is due to an absence of crimes, as if there existed one enchanted wood of innocence in the big, dark forest of Brazil's chronically degraded system.

If presidents, senators, and governors have corrupted and been corrupted, as Car Wash and other operations have so amply shown, it is impossible to believe that the same has not occurred at the higher courts, stocked as they are with political appointees.

The most important thing to avoid is that the higher courts become a sort of "safe haven" for the politico-corporate criminal organizations that have been leeching off public funds for decades. That is the battle that will rage for many years to come and before those very tribunals. So long as the superior and Supreme courts remain more committed to maintaining the power of oligarchs than serving the interests of the nation, Brazil runs a very real risk of seeing the efforts of recent years come to nothing.

In this context, the legal debate as to whether or not sentences should begin after a conviction is upheld by the first appellate court is crucial to the efficacy of the fight against impunity. Ever since the current constitution was promulgated in 1988, this discussion has returned time and again to the Supreme Court.

The case of former president Luiz Inácio Lula da Silva was about much more than simply jailing the ringleader of an institutionalized criminal organization, no matter how high a mandate he had once held. It was about precedent and the future of impunity. When his conviction was upheld by the fourth Federal District Court on January 24, 2018, his sentencing brought to a close the first phase of Operation Car Wash. But the debate as to whether he should or could be jailed while further appeals were possible became a pitched battle between those who wanted to eradicate impunity and those who wanted to eradicate Lava Jato.

His imprisonment would be—and in fact became—a milestone in the fight against the chronic inefficiency of our criminal system. And in the weeks preceding it, the Supreme Court split into two distinct factions, dubbed the "*punitivistas*" (who wanted to see the sentence served) and the "*garantistas*" (who wanted Lula to remain free all the way to the last of many possible appeals).[2]

Tense discussions ensued between the two camps, and it became crystal clear that the so-called *garantistas* would go to any lengths to keep Lula and other political heavyweights out of jail. So a lot more hung on the decision than the fate of one man. Supreme Court minister Gilmar Mendes—pontificating for the *garantistas*—among other ministers, seemed more intent on avoiding the *effects* Lula's imprisonment would have than the former president's jailing in itself.

On the other hand, the camp led by the ministers Luís Roberto Barroso and Edson Fachin had, throughout Operation Car Wash, adopted a position against protecting the nation's political elites.

Barroso, for example, has long contended that Car Wash brought to light once and for all an "oligarchic pact to sack the Brazilian State" and suggested, in session, that the *garantistas* were out to defend that pact. On March 21, 2018, during a heated exchange with Gilmar Mendes, Barroso lost his patience and declared that Mendes "had no ideas, no patriotism and [was] serving interests that had nothing to do with Justice," adding that his colleague was "a horrible person [. . .] with more than a hint of psychopathy" to his character.

The president's power to appoint a minister to the Supreme Court is a prerogative that reinforces the sense that those who ought to be totally independent of politicians embroiled in scandals are, in fact, beholden to them. As the appointment is practically for life (with mandatory retirement at seventy-five), a grateful Supreme Court judge can become a lasting problem when it comes to autonomy between the powers.

Some judges are appointed early in their careers, while still in their forties, for example, so they have three whole decades before them as ministers of the highest court in the land. Where a congressman or senator can be removed by the electorate after a four-year mandate, there is no such remedy for an ill-advised or ill-intentioned appointment to the higher courts, so the damage can go on for a lot longer.

One way of minimizing the nefarious effects of this is to do away with political appointments to the higher courts. However, that can only be done through a constitutional amendment. It may seem utopian to expect the political elite to show goodwill to society and relinquish the right to appoint their own firemen where the fight against impunity is fought most viciously, but it is absolutely imperative that society pressures its elected officials to do just that. And if that is perhaps a step too far for the political class, the least society can settle for would be the introduction of limited mandates for such appointments. More than any other, the capacity to appoint superior court judges with life tenure is the knot that most urgently needs to be untied if we are to bring down the safety net that currently breaks the fall of white-collar criminals.

A System Made Not to Work

Once the FP and public prosecutors' office had concluded most of their Car Wash investigations, and those indicted had been tried and convicted in the lower courts, new obstacles to the fight against corruption began to appear. This time, the establishment could not simply annul the investigations as they had done before, so many of those involved who did not have Supreme Court privilege ended up in cautionary detention through courageous trial-judge decisions.

But it was once the appeals began that the nation was reminded of the most chronic bug in its justice system. For those who can afford it, the appeals process is labyrinthine, and it can take years to navigate. This endless right to appeal is what keeps white-collar impunity going in Brazil, and we will not be able to surmount this obstacle without legislative change. Be that as it may, we can make do with the framework we have so long as the constitution is interpreted in society's favor, but that, as we have seen, is not always the case.

The crux of the issue is the debate concerning precisely when a sentence should begin. Is it once the conviction is upheld by the first collegiate court, after which the evidence presented in the case is no longer revisited and the ruling cannot be reversed on the grounds of merit? Or is it only once every possible route of appeal has been exhausted, all the way to the Supreme Court, a process that can be dragged out to extinctive prescription? By way of example we might mention the case of congressman Paulo Maluf, accused of embezzling municipal funds while mayor of São Paulo between 1993 and 1996. By the time his case was heard by the Supreme Court in 2017, Maluf was already eighty-six.[3] Minister Edson Fachin sentenced the congressman to almost eight years in prison, but fellow minister Dias Toffoli converted the sentence to house arrest only three months later.

In 2016, after intense debate, the STF determined that sentences should be served after a ruling by the first appellate court, but this short-lived jurisprudence was reversed in 2019 on the grounds of a "false *garantismo*" that alleged the sanctity of the presumption of innocence.

Of course, presuming innocence after the merit of the case has been judged and the defendant has been found guilty not once, but twice, is mere sophism. In the vast majority of democracies around the world, convicts start serving their sentences after the first unsuccessful appeal and in some countries even before that. In Brazil, for those who can afford good counsel, the right to appeal is guaranteed, no matter how frivolous the grounds.

The problem is that the Brazilian Constitution permits some room for interpretation. The letter of Item LVII of Article 5, Chapter 1, of the constitution reads that "no one shall be considered guilty before the issuing of a final and unappealable penal sentence," but it says nothing about jail time. In 2016, the Supreme Court reached the understanding that the execution of a sentence after a conviction is upheld by the first collegiate appellate court does not offend the presumption of innocence as this is where consideration of the evidence ends. A ruling of guilt delivered by a judge and corroborated by a panel of judges was deemed sufficient reason to no longer presume innocence.

Extending presumption of innocence to the higher courts is an artificial means of imposing impunity. In these cases, the *"garantismo"* is intended merely to prolong the penal process and stave off the final ruling for as long as possible, as Brazilian law allows for an infinity of appeals. The impression this leaves is that for the wealthy or powerful criminal, the "final and unappealable penal sentence" mentioned in the constitution never actually arrives, and jail time never begins.

And it's not a case of defending an irrational "punitivism" or social vengeance, as many in the legal profession contend, or of disrespecting human and legal rights. It's a question of ridding the nation of a debilitating impunity. The most important thing about these convictions is their prophylactic effect as a deterrent to corruption. Put in reverse, if corrupt politicians and businesspeople never come to trial, or there are endless delays in delivering a final judgment, what disincentive do they have to go on stealing?

On this point, too, the United States serves as a good model. The investigations conducted into the FIFA scandal—of major relevance in Brazil as it involved many key figures in the national and international game—proved the importance of speed and efficiency in legal processes. Administrators identified as members of a group specializing in embezzling funds from the sale of the TV rights to football sporting events were hit with hefty sentences and penalties under US financial crime legislation. José Maria Marin, former president of the Brazilian Football Confederation (CBF), was arrested on the day the operation was launched in Switzerland and remains in prison in the United States to this day. In addition to jail time, he was ordered to pay substantial fines.

In Brazil, the appeals bonanza allows the penal process to drag on indefinitely, a situation complicated still further by the fact that superior court judges are political appointees, turning the third and fourth tiers of the judiciary into "undoers" of justice, reversing trial-court rulings, and delaying processes until the statute of limitations has expired. All of this is profoundly disheartening and frustrating for Brazilian society.

The system seems built not to work, an unequal tug-of-war between investigators, prosecutors, and lower-court judges, on one side, and higher-court appointees committed to protecting the elites of politics, business, and the judiciary, on the other.

Besides the didactic effect of justice being served and embezzled public funds being recovered, improving our punitive system would have the indirect effect of deterring these crimes in the future. The appeals labyrinth is a multimillion-dollar industry for lawyers. If the benefits of this defective system only fall within the grasp of those who can afford to pay "good" attorneys, they also inflate the price of those services, with the fees rising in accordance with the level of access the defender claims to have to members of the judiciary.

A boutique lawyer can charge tens of millions of reais from a powerful politician or businessperson embroiled in a major corruption probe. And they don't much care where the money comes from. Naturally, the fees increase the higher, the case escalates—not to mention the success fees charged on concessions such as injunctions. In cases involving individuals shown to have been involved in massive kickback and corruption schemes, how can we be sure the vast sums paid to their lawyers are not the proceeds of crime? It's an industry that thrives on impunity derived from the laxity of our laws. Rowing against the international tide, the Brazilian Bar Association has refused to discuss the use of ill-gotten gains to pay legal fees. Regulations that would oblige legal professionals to inform the Brazilian Council for Financial Activities Control (COAF) of suspect communications, even if only in cases of consultancy, have still not made it off the drawing board.

Rather than discuss the minutiae of cases, construct compelling legal arguments, and endeavor to defend their clients' innocence on questions of merit, many of Brazil's leading criminal lawyers have specialized in legal trickery that doesn't necessarily lead to anyone being absolved of wrongdoing but merely delays the process ad nauseam, all the way to extinctive prescription, if possible. They are also skilled in the dark arts of having evidence thrown out and whole cases annulled. Unfortunately, the lethargy and complacency of the Brazilian justice system play in their favor.

Here, the devil is not in the details but in the framework. There's no point in blaming the lawyers for exploiting loopholes. The 2016 interpretation of Item LVII of Article 5, Chapter 1, of the constitution—despite the fact that it was reversed in 2019—shows that we can make progress in the way we apply our laws even without constitutional change.

And that's why Brazil's defense lawyers are so insistent on the new interpretation standing ad infinitum, because without it they could no longer trade so lucratively on the possibility of extinctive prescription or the concession of bail pending appeal after appeal after appeal. Of course, without such guarantees, defendants will think twice about forking out such exorbitant sums.

However, this overgenerous right to appeal is not the only cause of Brazil's impunity. Supreme Court privilege is another, and it applies to a surprisingly large number of people: 58,660 to be precise, according to a *Folha de S.Paulo* newspaper report.[4]

Of those granted Supreme Court privilege by the constitution, judges account for the largest individual block: 24,659.

Next are public prosecutors and defenders at state and federal levels: 18,412 in all.

The nation's mayors, at 5,570, make up the third-largest contingent, followed by State Assembly members, all 1,059 of them.

Other groups include congressmen (513), senators (81), officers of the armed forces (393), governors (27), Supreme Court judges (11), and, of course, the president.

In total, the occupants of 6,181 federal posts enjoy Supreme Court privilege.

Attempts have been made to change this. In May 2018, the Senate supported a Supreme Court initiative that would have restricted this privilege to the president, vice-president, senators, members of Congress, and, naturally, the Supreme Court itself. The initiative ran aground at the Lower House.

The situation becomes even more serious when we look toward the higher courts. According to a study by the magazine *Congresso em Foco*, of the 500 senators and members of Congress brought before the superior and Supreme courts since 1988, only 16 were convicted of any wrongdoing. In other words, the higher courts are a "safe haven" for institutionalized crime. Former president Fernando Collor, for example, faced three charges at the Supreme Court for crimes committed in 1992: presenting false evidence, bribery, and embezzlement. The first two charges reached extinctive prescription before the case came to trial—twenty-two years later—and the third was thrown out for lack of evidence.

This Supreme Court "sanctuary" has never been so hotly disputed than in recent years, when it has proved the salvation of numerous authorities.

Institutionalized Crime as a Threat to the Nation's Development

As if the billions of Brazilian Reais syphoned off in corruption schemes weren't bad enough in themselves, institutionalized crime causes even more serious damage to the nation by delaying its development. In terms of sheer perniciousness, there is no mafia that can compare with a criminal organization that occupies the nation's institutions and wields the power to create taxes, draft budgets, appoint authorities, and approve laws.

Conceptually speaking, we see four major problems caused by systemic corruption:

1. The direct damage is done to democracy by institutionalized crime within the legislature. This rot takes hold as soon as the legislative process—proposing bills, passing laws, and delivering speeches to the floor—is perverted and vitiated by the interests of criminal groups. A substantial portion of the bills that reach the Lower and Upper houses were neither drafted nor submitted for the good of society but to serve the private interests of those who finance corruption and our contaminated and degraded electoral system. What we see time and again is a form of systemic legislative fraud, because not only do our legislators produce laws in the service of shady interests, but they neglect to work toward refining our legal framework. In other words, not only do they do what they shouldn't, they don't do what they should, and the result is our deterioration as a nation.

2. As soon as major projects are approved for their "corruption value," the national interest and future is once again sabotaged. All too often, graft is the star by which our national course is set. Clear examples of this are the mega-events Brazil undertook in 2014 and 2016—the FIFA World Cup and the Olympic Games, respectively. Dozens of stadia and other sports facilities were built for these events without any need whatsoever, seeing as there were adequate existing venues that could have been used or revamped instead. The country had countless priorities to attend to ahead of this kind of national chest-puffing, but the opportunity for major kickbacks on such vast construction projects won the day.

The choice of where certain World Cup stadia were built was unjustifiable from the start, according to an assessment conducted by Pluri Consultoria, which studied Brazil's World Cup "legacy." Basing its calculations on average ticket sales and state championship revenues between 2013 and 2018, the study found that it would take the stadiums constructed in the Distrito Federal, Mato Grosso, and Amazonas (none of which have first-division teams in the National League) many thousands of years to recoup the investment lavished on their construction for just a handful of World Cup games. In the case of the National Stadium in the Distrito Federal, it would take 216,343 games, or 2,739 years, before the stadium broke even. The Pantanal Arena in Mato Grosso was somewhat better, but it would still require

69,310 games and 1,216 years before any profit whatsoever was seen. The Amazon Arena, for its part, would have to host 118,673 games over 3,207 years in order to justify its construction.

Stadium data

	Distrito Federal	Mato Grosso	Amazonas
Stadium	Estádio Nacional	Arena Pantanal	Arena da Amazônia
City	Brasília	Cuiabá	Manaus
Investment (R$ millions)	1,704	646	670
Seating capacity	69,349	41,390	44,351
Cost per seat (R$)	24,571	15,611	15,095
Cost per seat (US$ average at time of construction)	11,400	6,506	7,638
Ranking among world's most expensive stadia	2nd	24th	19th

State championships—Last six editions (2013/2018)

	Distrito Federal	Mato Grosso	Amazonas
Number of games	464	369	359
Average attendance	1,150	709	486
Revenue per game (R$)	7,876	9,322	5,642
Profit per game (R$)	1,826	1,615	282
Lowest attendance	8	12	2
Games with fewer than 100 supporters	52	44	83
Games with profits under R$ 1,000	98	24	82
% of games with under 1,000 paying supporters	76	80	88
Average ticket price per supporter (R$)	6.85	13.15	11.62
State championship games needed to recoup investment*	216,343	69,310	118,673
Years required to recoup investment*	2,739	1,216	3,207

Note: Available at: <www.oantagonista.com/brasil/veja-por-que-o-legado-da-copa-deveria-parar-no-delegado/>. Accessed on: January 15th 2019

*Figures are purely illustrative, considering the unreal hypothesis that all profits would go toward amortizing the investment and not factoring in maintenance costs or depreciation.

Source: Study by Pluri Consultoria. O antagonista, "Veja por que o 'legado' da Copa deveria parar no delegado," 26 abr. 2018. Available at: <www.oantagonista.com/brasil/veja-por-que-o-legado-da-copa-deveria-parar-no-delegado/>. Accessed on: January 25, 2019.

Sport is not the only area in which major projects are undertaken on the back of their corruptibility. The same happens in priority areas too, such as the construction of oil refineries. On this score, the Abreu e Lima refinery in Pernambuco is a classic example.[5] According to financial crimes experts at the Federal Police in Curitiba, the refinery will never be able to make back the money spent on its construction. Unfortunately, the only reason it was built in the first place was to generate kickbacks.

3. "Custo Brasil":[6] A euphemism for the added cost heaped onto something by the simple fact that it was done in Brazil, where systemic corruption and inefficiency have to be factored into any endeavor. It encompasses the overpricing and price-padding of practically everything purchased by the Treasury. As the money that irrigates corruption schemes ultimately comes from the public coffers, "custo Brasil" is, in effect, the cost of the nation's corruption passed down per capita. After all, the bill lands with the taxpayer.
4. Corrosion of citizenship and civic responsibility: The average Brazilian does not trust the nation's institutions, and this does huge damage to national pride. Most Brazilians feel helpless to change the state of things and that saps any motivation they may have had to try. People have no faith whatsoever in the system, in all its manifestations. Even the electronic urns used at the elections are looked upon with distrust.[7] The endless succession of scandals, absurd delay in any penal process coming to completion, and the general sense of impunity form a vicious circle that leads to an overbearing feeling of impotence. In the long term, the resulting low self-esteem and disbelief in the system could lead to widespread disregard for the law and create a whole generation with no commitment whatsoever to society and no will to change the status quo.

Chapter 12

PROPOSALS FOR THE FUTURE

If the followers of the law are strong, the nation will be strong; if the followers of the law are weak, the nation will be weak.

Han Fei, Chinese philosopher (280–233 BCE)

Jorge Pontes and Márcio Anselmo: We're facing a type of crime that has entrenched itself in the structures of power, where it is perpetrated from top to bottom and inside out. Despite the positive results Operation Car Wash has obtained in recent years, we still do not have the legal instruments and institutional protections needed to defend society against the illicit actions of our corrupt political and business elites. The state needs to structure itself so that we don't slip back into the kind of status quo where this criminal modality can take root again.

Institutionalized crime occupies the most powerful positions in the land and wields the authority to appoint ministers, state company directors, police commissioners, high-court judges, federal and state auditors, and the directors who oversee the work of our prosecutors and investigators and who also, and extremely importantly, control their budgets. The agents of institutionalized crime hold elected office that permits them to propose, discuss, vote, and promulgate laws that shield them from prosecution, protect the funds they embezzle, and persecute those who investigate and attempt to indict them. And from the benches of the highest courts in the land, they can control and neutralize the criminal cases brought against their mandated mafiosos.

Institutionalized crime pervades the three powers of the republic and tilts the field of battle in its own favor. What we have seen in recent years is a cycle in which institutionalized crime, having reached its zenith, has become so omnipresent it can draft public policy tailored to its nefarious designs, implement that policy through the legislature (as law) or executive (as decree), devise the mechanisms by which it is controlled, and even rule on its legality and their own immunity before the criminal justice system.

There is simply no rescuing a hijacked state without legal and structural institutional changes being made. How can we invest against a criminal system that has the power to handpick our bosses, slash our budgets, pass the laws that regulate our work, and appoint the judges who will try their cases? Under these circumstances, the chances of success are negligible.

Having identified and named this new species of criminal fauna— the whale that, until recently, we only ever glimpsed in snatches before it dove once again into the murky depths—we present some proposals that could help rebuild our governmental structure and wrestle back the reins of the state.

Our decades of experience within the Federal Police enables us to identify some administrative measures that, from a structural point of view, would allow the FP to gain significant ground in terms of heightened potential for action and efficacy in combatting white-collar crime in Brazil.

The first of these would be to create a unit specializing in the investigation of large-scale, high-level embezzlements of public funds, analyzing federal expenditure with a view to detecting fraud in public tenders and the execution of major contracts. This initiative could also involve a unit with expertise in construction engineering and forensic accounting, trained to find the devils in the details. Developing know-how in this area is a daunting challenge for the FP. Even today, five years into Operation Car Wash, fraudsters continue to rig bids, arrange kickbacks, and inflate prices. And this can go on largely because it's a kind of fraud that remains hard to detect.

Another fundamental change needed is to put an end to the constant expansion of the Federal Police's remit. All too often new attributions are piled on without much thought or planning and without recruiting new personnel qualified for the tasks in hand. There are various bills of law out there that would see the Judiciary Police—the FP—snowed under with all sorts of new duties and focuses, such as the repression of armed militias and paramilitary organizations, investigation of crimes against journalists, internal drug trafficking, and even hate crimes against women. These are all important areas that require solid policing, but they cannot be designated exclusively to the Federal Police, and attempts to do so are motivated by only one thing: an interest in diluting FP resources and distracting attention away from mega-operations like Car Wash. Rather than pass the buck, the best way to give the areas above the attention they deserve would be to strengthen the investigative capacity of the Civil Police.

It is also essential that periodical entrance exams be held to ensure there is a steady and timely influx of new recruits to replace retiring, resigning, or transferred Federal Police personnel. To avoid understaffing, new rounds of entrance examinations should be held automatically every time a certain number of vacant positions becomes available. Establishing a minimum acceptable headcount floor would be an easy way to eliminate the endless red tape surrounding requisitions for new hires. In this sense, also key is a change of mindset. The Federal Police needs to be seen not as a drain on resources but as an investment, given its potential returns to the state through corruption thwarted and ill-gotten assets seized and retrieved.

We also propose that the FP be relieved of its administrative duties so that it can focus on becoming a specialist police force with its own budget and financial autonomy. Passport administration, border control, regulation, and inspection of private security firms, among other functions, could all be transferred to other organs or to a new organ created especially for those ends while leaving the Federal Police in charge of managing the related data streams.

On the other hand, it is also crucial that the FP be endowed with central authority in all international criminal cooperation, in the molds of the current Department for International Asset Recovery and Legal Cooperation (DRCI), so that it can handle its requests directly with other nations. At a time when the concealment of illicit assets abroad has become a speciality among criminal organizations that filch state funds, strengthening cooperation with other countries and international organizations is absolutely key, and bringing this under the FP's purview would reduce the potential influence of institutionalized crime in such a vital area.

In addition to recovering assets abroad, the de-capitalization of criminal structures domestically is another essential means of discouraging this kind of crime.

The harder it becomes to enjoy the fruits of corruption, the less interesting an option it becomes. Achieving more agility and efficiency in rooting out money-laundering schemes and beefing up our means of prevention are therefore of the utmost importance if we are to ensure that crime does not pay.

Continuing on this line, the Civil Police departments must also be structured and trained to pursue this kind of criminality, which is just as damaging on a regional scale as it is on a federal level.

Another area that needs buttressing is internal affairs, starting with the transfer of IA Departments to premises outside the police precinct.

Harsher punishments must be meted out to police officers who allow themselves to be corrupted, and it is essential that internal affairs investigations be reinforced and given the priority they deserve.

Our present accountability measures require a lot more work if they are to present transparent and accurate quantitative and qualitative data on police performance. Transparency must be the guiding star of our State of Law, because the population has the right to know the return it is getting on the tax revenues invested in all branches of the civil service, the police forces included. Lastly, another positive measure would be to stop leasing federal agents out to other organs and, particularly, as aides to senators, congressmen, and ministers. Politics is not an area that requires, or should have any access to, Federal Police resources. Only the Ministry of Justice, Public Security Departments, and international organs combatting globalized organized crime have any legitimate need for FP personnel.

A second batch of proposals concerns legislative changes, but we are aware that these are harder to implement. Nevertheless, they are also the measures that would have the most impact in terms of restructuring the Brazilian state. The first of these would be to make the Federal Police director-general's post a mandated appointment, limited to one four-year term, beginning halfway through the presidential mandate. This change would attenuate the president of the republic's influence on the post, as the incumbent's term would straddle two separate presidential mandates. The director-general should also be selected from a three-name shortlist supplied by a superior college of Federal Police chiefs. The fact that the four-year mandate is nonrenewable would avoid the politicking that goes with canvassing for reappointment, so director-generals would not be tempted to enter into any quid pro quo.

A constitutional amendment should be passed to prohibit the political appointment of judges to the state and federal courts, Superior Court of Justice (STJ), and Supreme Court (STF). The regional and federal courts would be stocked with career magistrates, chosen in accordance with objective criteria by a collegiate panel composed of chief justices—state, regional, or federal—depending on the posts to be filled. Members of the STJ and STF would be recruited solely from the ranks of chief justices and serve nonrenewable ten-year mandates. This prohibition on political appointments should also extend to the auditors' courts, whose justices would be recruited through public entrance examinations only, while all advisory positions would be occupied by career civil servants from the appropriate organs.

Along similar lines, we argue in favor of eradicating posts by appointment on state boards and directorates. Presidential, gubernatorial, and mayoral appointments would be limited to their cabinets, that is, ministers and department secretaries. Directorial and managerial positions at public and semi-state companies would be filled by duly qualified civil servants, thus avoiding the current use of cushy, strategic posts in the public apparatus as currency in political alliance-building.

In terms of criminal law, one prophylactic measure would be a suite of legislation that takes a far harder line on crimes of corruption involving the occupants of public positions. Such crimes should be classified as felonies with nonparolable mandatory minimum sentences.

Wading into a debate that is gaining more and more space in Brazilian society, for a number of reasons, we believe it is essential that we revive the discussion on the gradual decriminalization of drugs. The way it is approached under our present legislation, the war on narcotics, has proved ineffective and, indeed, damaging. The negatives are manifold: it fuels the formation of ghettos and presidios of violence in underprivileged, densely populated areas, exacerbates street-level crime, fosters a screed of collateral misdemeanors and felonies, feeds weapons dealing and police corruption, and overburdens the penitentiary system with tens of thousands of youths accused or convicted of minor crimes. No less importantly, it distracts FP attention and resources away from what should be the corporation's core mission: effectively combatting major corruption.

POSTSCRIPT
ABOUT A PLANE

It was early morning on September 26, 2016, when I, Márcio Anselmo, left my hotel near Rua Augusta, downtown São Paulo, and joined the rest of the Curitiba team as we made our way to the FP Superintendency on the Tietê beltway. The previous day we had departed from Curitiba with the mission of launching Operation Omertà,[1] the thirty-fifth phase of Car Wash. Our prime target was none other than Lula's former minister of finance and Dilma's ex-chief of staff, Antonio Palocci.

The operation was the result of painstaking investigative work by Police Chief Filipe Pace, who had uncovered the now-legendary "Amigo" spreadsheet, detailing a whole list of bribe payments made to former president Lula and numerous other figures, all attributed creative code names.[2]

On that Monday, we set out at 3:30 a.m. and were all tooled up and gathered in the FP São Paulo auditorium a little over fifteen minutes later. Two hours after that, warrants in hand, we departed in convoy for Palocci's address in the swanky Jardins neighborhood.

As is customary on such operations, we arrived at 6:00 a.m., with the sun rising. We informed the porter of our business and were shown to Palocci's apartment, which occupied a whole floor of an upscale building. A few moments later, we rang the doorbell.

When the door was answered, we presented our warrants and entered the property. Palocci had long known this day would come, even if he couldn't tell precisely when.

Standing in his majestic residence, the former PT luminary was read his rights and taken off to Curitiba. On October 25, 2016, Police Chief Pace closed this phase of his investigations, from which he drew the following conclusions:

According to Judiciary Police Analysis Report 675/2016 (Event 54, Annex 6, Files 5043559- 60.2016.4.04.7000), LUIZ INÁCIO LULA DA SILVA was known by the codenames "FRIEND OF MY FATHER" and "FRIEND OF EO,"[3] when referred to by MARCELO

BAHIA ODEBRECHT, and as "FRIEND OF YOUR FATHER" and "FRIEND OF EO," when referred to by interlocutors of MARCELO BAHIA ODEBRECHT.

While there is ample evidence to conclude, and with investigative coherency, that the "friend" referred to in spreadsheets "POSITION—ITALIANO 310712MO.xls" and "POSITION—ITALIANO 22 OCT 2013 TO 25 NOV.xls" is LUIZ INÁCIO LULA DA SILVA, investigating the former President's criminal responsibility lies outside the jurisdiction of GT LAVA JATO, of which this Police Authority is a part. It is hereby noted, however, that the above mentioned probatory elements have been brought to the attention of Federal Police Chief MÁRCIO ADRIANO ANSELMO, in charge of the investigation under which, in theory, any illicit acts perpetrated by LUIZ INÁCIO LULA DA SILVA would fall.

From what could be ascertained, ANTONIO PALOCCI FILHO was the true overseer of the bribery payments made by ODEBRECHT and registered in the spreadsheets "POSITION—ITALIANO 310712MO.xls" and "POSITION—ITALIANO 22 OCT 2013 EM 25 NOV.xls."

In a deposition under oath on September 6, 2017, Palocci was categorical in affirming that the relationship between the construction group Odebrecht and the Lula and Dilma governments was fueled by bribes. Sometime later, in 2018, Palocci sealed a plea-bargain testimony agreement with the Federal Police, coordinated by Police Chief Pace and ratified by the Fourth District Court in Porto Alegre on June 22 that same year.

While the spreadsheets were extremely illustrative of the concept of institutionalized crime, perhaps nothing has proved quite so emblematic of the theory developed in this book than certain facts that emerged early in 2019, namely that Lula had used the presidential airplane— *Aerolula*, as it was called—to transport bribe payments received in specie. Even if the authorities never manage to obtain concrete proof to corroborate Palocci's declarations, we believe he had far more reason to be truthful than to lie, as any false testimony on his part would send him straight back to jail.[4]

The facts as recounted by Palocci form the most elucidating allegory we have found thus far for institutionalized crime. Until then, we had not come across anything that expressed so well the idea of an ineradicable mafia organization controlled by people at the very center of power who use the instruments and official property of the republic to criminal ends.

Just as they used the *Official Gazette* to appoint professional fraudsters to key Petrobras posts, they availed of the presidential plane, Brazil's Air Force One, complete with all its official security, to transport bribe money. It's the epitome of institutionalized corruption.

Of course, no Federal Police crew, or any other police force, would be able to intercept anything transported aboard the presidential airplane, not even cash bribes intermediated by the minister of finance on the orders of the commander in chief himself. It's the perfect crime in its most crystalline form.

The pen that signs and the hands that wield it, the cabinets in which those individuals sit, the *Official Gazette* that publishes their decisions, the congressional votes that approve laws, and now even the plane that ferries the executive across Brazil's skies, none of it escapes corrupt misappropriations. Using BAF 001—a French-built airbus requisitioned by Lula early in his first mandate—to transport the proceeds of corruption is the quintessence of institutionalized crime.

After all these discoveries, we cannot afford to delude ourselves into thinking that institutionalized crime can be completely eradicated. It has the power to conceal itself and to grow back in other forms, dressed up as something not immediately recognizable. It is more than capable of disguising itself and passing its heirs off as the soldiers of probity.

To defeat it, one of the most effective weapons we have as a society is the cultivation of a very long and indelible memory, so that we can see through the fallacies systematically spun by the operators of a vast criminal organization.

AFTERWORD

THE NORMALIZATION OF MALFEASANCE: WHY IT'S SO HARD TO DISMANTLE INSTITUTIONALIZED CRIME IN BRAZIL

Luís Roberto Barroso

The two Federal Police commissioners who authored this book were responsible for operations that have changed the Brazilian reality in terms of combatting corruption. Reading it bestows a genuine immersion in recent Brazilian history that leaves the reader with a paradoxical sensation of despair and hope—despair at the atavistically entrenched venality of the nation's ruling elites; hope at the simple realization that when the right people fill the right posts, the nation can shed many of the stigmas of its past and progress toward a far more worthy destination. The feeling that we are chronically led by the worst of a bad lot gradually gives way to a burgeoning belief that there are good people out there too and that redemption lies in their getting into a position from which they can prevail.

Despite the age difference between them, Jorge Pontes and Márcio Anselmo belong to a technically endowed, vocationally oriented generation of Federal Police agents that has worked a lasting revolution in how corruption is policed in Brazil. The stories told in this book are first-hand testimonies to the fact that there is more to the public sector than unserviceable queues, delays, red tape, and inefficiency. They are also living proof that serious work and persistence can garner significant change even within the most rigid, bureaucratic public structures.

Brazil's levels of corruption are not the product of individual lapses or all-too-human failings. What we now see is a brand of corruption that is structural and systemic, infecting a sprawling arc of alliances that spans private and state-run companies, key business figures, civil servants of all ranks, political parties (of all colors), and members of the executive and the legislature. We have consistently seen professionally operated graft schemes capable of syphoning off and distributing crippling volumes of public funds. As I have so often said, it is impossible not to blush with shame at what has taken place among us. These schemes have become the standard form of doing politics and business in Brazil. At the top of the political pyramid, this wholesale corruption derived from an *oligarchic pact* sealed between influential swathes of the political, business, and civil-service classes and designed to sack the Treasury and, by extension, steal from the pockets of the Brazilian taxpayer. The Brazilian state has been hijacked by, and bent to serve, private interests.

In recent years, society has stirred from its decades-long lethargy and begun to demand integrity, idealism, and patriotism from its elected and appointed officials. And this energy has started to change paradigms and steer history. The social backlash has driven important changes of attitude that are starting to resonate among the institutions, legislation, and jurisprudence. Chief among these changes is an end to the deeply engrained mafioso model of electoral campaign financing by major business interests, the drastic restriction of Supreme Court privilege, and the fact that prison terms can now be enforced once convictions are upheld by the first collegiate court. All of these advances were fiercely resisted. Our backwardness is by no means accidental. It was carefully crafted and is staunchly defended by those who have long profited from it.

It is a terrible mistake to assume that corruption is not a violent crime. Corruption kills. It kills patients in public health-service queues, waiting for beds that don't exist and medicines that have not been bought. It kills on badly maintained highways. It destroys lives that have not received adequate education due to a paucity of schools, structural deficiencies, and lack of equipment. The fact that the corrupt don't look their victims in the eye as they do their damage does not make them any less dangerous. Belief that corruption is a lesser crime has created a general atmosphere of leniency and impunity that has put us in the mire we find ourselves in today, a toxic mixture of economic recession, corruption, and rampant criminality that pulls us down as a country, trapped within an absurdly low average income, unable to gain traction.

Such impunity has resulted in a nation in which corruption is endemic: where high-level members of the executive negotiate kickbacks and bribes in the very government palaces from which they ought to be governing with dignity and probity, and where governors transform their gubernatorial seats into distribution centers for misappropriated public funds. Where congressmen and senators sell rebates and other fiscal breaks at premium rates, members of congressional investigation committees blackmail and extort people and companies under threat of subpoena and public humiliation. And where the directors of public financial institutions charge percentile fees on the loans they approve, the directors of public-company pension funds authorize ruinous investments in return for a cut of the sums disbursed.

Tackling corruption requires no punitivism or masked crusaders. We need neither Robespierre nor Savonarola. All it takes is the proper enforcement of the law, with none of the cronyism traditionally practiced by public figures who believe themselves to be above it. But it also requires defeating the two-faced partners of corruption, who lurk in the shadows of a strange phenomenon: Brazilian-style guarantism. In other parts of the world, guarantism means the protection of civil liberties, due legal process, a fair trial, and, in some places—though not all—right to higher court of appeal.

Among us, however, there are some who defend a distorted brand of guarantism that effectively amounts to an acquired right to impunity afforded by a penal process that doesn't work, seldom ends, and never affects anyone who earns more than a few times the minimum wage. These tropical *guarantistes* mercilessly condemn and imprison underprivileged youths with no prior convictions caught in possession of the smallest quantities of drugs, but trot out fustian libertarian discourses to justify the acquittal of corrupt politicians and businessmen who aren't even forced to hand back the cash they have spirited away into offshore accounts.

Brazil is ranked 105th in Transparency International's 2018 Corruption Perceptions Index. We are the world's fourth-largest democracy, one of the ten biggest economies on the planet, but we languish among the worst of the worst when it comes to governmental integrity. Fewer than 1 percent of our prison inmates are white-collar criminals. The figures are frankly embarrassing. But Brazilian society has changed, and things will never be the same again. We are moving in the right direction now, albeit not as quickly as we would like. It will fall to the next generation to complete the work begun by the likes of Jorge Pontes and Márcio Anselmo. And this book leaves no doubt whatsoever: the time is now, the place is here.

This book serves as a crash course in how political criminality works in Brazil, offering a vivid description of the vicious cycle that sees political parties and their members perpetuate their hold on mandated power so that they can continue to bleed the nation for personal benefit. By defrauding public tenders or padding contracts with major campaign "donors," public money is misappropriated and used to grease the cogs of the mechanisms of corruption, enriching politicians, their appointees to cushy directorates, and the businesspeople who negotiate with them, boosting company profits while ensuring even more lavish donations for future campaigns.

Distinguishing this from traditional white-collar criminality, the authors coin the term "institutionalized crime"—a varied and highly lucrative system of frauds that worms its way into the kernel of power and into official public structures. Here we have violations perpetrated by people invested with formal authority, who use the prerogatives of their posts not only to commit crimes but to create a whole network of protection against investigation and penal prosecution. Unlike the modus operandi of traditional criminal organizations, institutionalized crime does not operate outside the law but right "inside it."

To illustrate their arguments, the authors draw upon their own concrete experience on the force and back it up with the works of respected sociologists. Their inside view of police operations enables them to draw a sadly realist portrait of how hitherto untouchable power-mongers manage to lay themselves a safety net of favors and intimidation that keeps the law at bay. Their tricks are myriad, including disinformation campaigns in the press, moving key FP personnel around like pawns on a board, and availing of "institutional leaks" to ensure they are tipped off ahead of police operations and can take steps to interfere with investigations or influence/handpick judges, and so on. With sophisticated perception and bruising language, the authors assert:

> Implicit to the notion that public property belongs to "no-one" as opposed to "everyone" is the logic that misappropriating it is therefore no grave matter.
>
> These schemes are supra-ideological, as they operate under governments right and left.
>
> Unlike the "conventional" criminal organization, institutionalized crime is not connected with blatantly illegal activities, such as drugs or weapons dealing, prostitution, human trafficking or illegal gambling. [. . .] On the contrary, it bores right into the official platform. It is infinitely more lucrative and secure than any conventional illegal business. The part the judicial institutions have played in consistently downgrading white-collar crime and corruption to mere misdemeanors does not escape the authors' scathing criticism either, and they are forthright in accusing the higher courts of pandering to political, personal and class ties and of blowing a protective bubble around well-connected members of the political and business elites.

The situation has begun to change, but continues to warrant a severe diagnosis and some caustic words of concern:

It is crucial that we prevent the higher Courts from functioning as a get-out-of-jail-free card for politico-corporate organizations that have spent decades leeching off the public coffers. This is a battle to be fought inside the courts themselves for many years to come. If the higher courts, such as the superior and supreme courts, remain more committed to protecting the oligarchs than the country itself, Brazil will continue to face a real risk of seeing all these recent efforts come to nothing.

Regarding the drugs issue, the authors argue against the grain and defend an essential change of tack in how the question is handled. With daring and eloquence, they eschew the general prejudices and cut straight to what will certainly become obvious to most in the future:

In a debate that is gaining ever more space and importance in society, for various reasons, it is important to pick up the thread of the gradual decriminalization of drugs in Brazil. The way the war on narcotics is approached in our current anti-drugs legislation has proved ineffective and the driver of various negative consequences: it propels and deepens ghettoization and the creation of war zones in densely-populated underprivileged areas; it fuels street crime; generates dozens of corollary crimes, such as weapons dealing and police corruption; and suffocates the penitentiary system with tens of thousands of young prisoners jailed for drug-related misdemeanors. And, no less important, it distracts the Federal Police (FP) from what should be its core mission: effectively and robustly combatting large-scale corruption.

The authors are not content merely to diagnose the various problems they identify across the board, and in the closing chapter they propose concrete solutions, ranging from more efficient investigative mechanisms and greater autonomy for the FP to legislative changes against impunity. The reader may disagree here or there, as is only healthy in a world of plural opinions and points of view, but, in general, Jorge Pontes and Márcio Anselmo are on the right side of history here, and they defend their ideas with talent and courage.

The simple existence of this book is already an extremely positive sign of transformation and progress. It is no coincidence that both of its authors began their careers in narcotics, which continues to be the main focus of Brazilian penal repression, but realized early on the terrible cost-benefit relation of this Sisyphean battle.[1] There are no winners in the war on drugs.

When we stop criminalizing users and arresting small-time dealers, begin to regulate the use of less dangerous drugs and those of medicinal value, and start employing intelligence to cut off the financial conduits to major drug lords, then we will be making a far more advantageous deployment of the resources at our disposal. Tackling narcotics better, and higher up the supply chain, as the authors argue, will free up time and resources for the real wars on our hands, namely against political corruption, the misappropriation of public funds, money-laundering, and environmental crime. Now that we have some measure of the sheer magnitude of institutionalized crime in Brazil, we need to channel resources and effort into taking it down. It's past time we revised our penal priorities, and this book is an important step in that direction.

Brazil is undergoing something of a refounding, urged by a society that will no longer accept the unacceptable. It's a complex, fraught, and occasionally traumatic process of raising the ethical bar in both the public and private spheres, and though history will definitely need a helping shoulder to drive it on, we must have the humility to recognize that time needs time. We cannot give up before the mission is accomplished. This book is part of the dynamic underway, ferrying the Brazilian institutions toward a more mature version of themselves. It is a valuable contribution toward a better and brighter nation.[*]

---

[*] Luís Roberto Barroso is a minister of the Federal Supreme Court, professor at the State University of Rio de Janeiro, and a senior fellow at Harvard Kennedy School.

NOTES

Chapter 1

1 Operation Acarajé was phase 23 of Operation Car Wash. It was named for the spicy prawn dumpling popular in Bahia, home state of the marketeer João Santana. In messages exchanged by Odebrecht staff, "acarajés" was code for "cash."

2 In April 2016, Janot filed an injunction with the Supreme Court demanding that the FP be prohibited from negotiating plea-bargain agreements without the involvement of the Public Prosecutors' Office.

Chapter 2

1 The *O Globo* Newspaper, March 16th 1997.

Chapter 3

1 From an article published in the news portal G1 on October 9, 2014, under the title "Youssef claims Lula caved under pressure to appoint Paulo Roberto Costa."

2 In a bid to stabilize rampant inflation, President Fernando Collor (1990–2) took the radical move of freezing prices, wages, and 80 percent of all Brazilian bank deposits for a period of eighteen months. The idea was to suffocate inflation by keeping money from circulating. The plan ultimately failed, having little real impact on inflation, which remained in the region of 20 percent per month.

3 The Portuguese term *doleiro* became common during Brazil's hyperinflation years in the 1980s, when people frequently resorted to black-market money changers so they could protect their savings from devaluation by converting them into dollars, a practice that was illegal at the time. The term is still used today, but for black-market bankers, like Youssef, who move money around the financial system, both internally and abroad, by illegal means. In light of this change, and in the interests of brevity, we have opted to translate the term *doleiro* as "money-mover."

4 During President Lula's first term of office (2002–5), a scheme was
set up to keep members of Congress on monthly retainer so that they
would vote with the government as needed. The scheme was nicknamed
Mensalão, the "big-monthly," and the stipend was generally R$30,000 per
congressman.

5 José Sarney was not elected president directly. He was handpicked as the
regime-friendly vice to President Tancredo Neves, the reformist elected
by indirect vote in 1985. Neves died before he could take office, so Sarney
ended up serving his term in his stead. Sarney has always been deeply
unpopular outside his home state of Maranhão, where his power has been
absolute for decades.

6 ¹⁰ In May 2017, the FP launched Operation Back on Track, which detected
the payment of bribes related to the railroad's construction.

7 The Brazilian Federal Police has regional superintendencies in the capital
cities of each of the federation's twenty-seven states.

Chapter 4

1 The only exception, of course, is the Judiciary Police, which reports
directly to the judiciary in executing search-and-arrest warrants and
escorting witnesses.

2 According to the Ministry of Justice data released in December 2017:
http://antigo.depen.gov.br/DEPEN/depen/sisdepen/infopen/relatorios
-sinteticos/infopen-dez-2016-rev-12072019-0802.pdf. Accessed on
January 4, 2019.

Chapter 5

1 Brazil's current anti–money-laundering legislation dates to 1998 and
was promulgated by then president of the republic Fernando Henrique
Cardoso (law no. 613/98).

2 United Nations Convention against Transnational Organized Crime, 2000,
p. 5.

3 Law no. 12,850 "defines a criminal organization and regulates criminal
investigations, the means by which evidence can be gathered, and what
constitutes a correlate criminal infraction and criminal investigative
procedure," August 2, 2013.

4 *Folha de S.Paulo*, "Joesley says that Cardozo regrets the law against
criminal organizations," September 29, 2017. In the dialogue, which
Joesley recounted to investigators, he allegedly says to Cardozo: "You
remember how happy you were, celebrating the law against organized
crime?" To which Cardozo responds: "An eeeepic fuck-up, Joesley. [. . .]

We passed that law thinking about organized crime, about the drugs trade. Man, Dilma and I really got that one wrong." His regret was apparently due to the use Operation Car Wash was making of that very law. Cardozo denied the conversation ever took place.

5 Cavalcanti made this request in May 2005.

6 The rapporteur of PLS-85 was Senator Roberto Requião (PMDB).

7 Presented by congressman Wadih Damous (PT) in 2016, the bill would have altered the existing Organized Crime Law in ways that would have defused Operation Car Wash.

8 The anticorruption unit, closed by gubernatorial decree on November 7, 2018, in the northeastern state of Pernambuco, was left with only forty-five days in which to wrap up five outstanding corruption investigations.

9 Zampronha's report was submitted in February 2011 and served as the bedrock for criminal action 470, brought the following year, as per the vote by the Supreme Court rapporteur, Joaquim Barbosa.

10 Chief of Staff Erenice Guerra was accused of influence peddling over government contracts celebrated with a company owned by her son. She resigned in September 2010. The investigation against her was dropped in 2012.

11 Four cases were heard against Gleisi Hoffmann at the Supreme Court. In June 2018, she was absolved of corruption and money laundering involving kickbacks on contracts with Petrobras. Three further accusations were brought against her by the Public Prosecutor's Office— two related to the receipt of bribes from Odebrecht and one for engaging in organized criminal activity.

12 Jaques Wagner was the target of Operation Red Card, in February 2018. Based on testimony from Odebrecht executives, the investigation looked into illegalities in the demolition and reconstruction of the Fonte Nova stadium in Salvador, Bahia, ahead of the 2014 World Cup.

13 Aloizio Mercadante was accused of receiving one million reais in illegal donations for his gubernatorial bid in São Paulo in 2010. The case was dropped in June 2018.

14 Eliseu Padilha was charged alongside former president Michel Temer and other members of the MDB party with engaging in organized criminal activity.

15 In 2005, when the mensalão case came to light during his term as justice minister, Thomaz Bastos invented a line of defense that admitted the circulation of illicit funds, but argued that these were "merely" irregular campaign donations, not bribes. In 2012, during the mensalão trial, he was the attorney defending the vice-chairman of Banco Rural, José Roberto Salgado. Commenting on the vote delivered by the rapporteur, Ricardo Lewandowski, who absolved some of the defendants on all counts of corruption, Thomaz Bastos was reported to have said that it was "a victory for the campaign-funding thesis." Reported by the *O Globo* and *O Estado de S. Paulo* newspapers on August 24.

16 When he presented his denunciations to the Supreme Court in September 2017, then attorney general Rodrigo Janot formalized two separate accusations of engaging in organized criminal activity: one against the Senate members of MDB (Edison Lobão, Jader Barbalho, Renan Calheiros, Romero Jucá, and Valdir Raupp) and another against the congressional members of MDB (Michel Temer, Eduardo Cunha, Henrique Alves, Geddel Vieira Lima, Rodrigo Loures, Eliseu Padilha, and Moreira Franco). As Janot understood it, they formed distinct criminal organizations.

17 *Folha de S.Paulo*, "Sérgio Motta brokered pro-reelection votes, says congressman," May 14, 1997. The May 13 report, which triggered the scandal, revealed the existence of a recording in which congressman Ronivon Santiago told a friend that he sold his vote to the pro-reelection camp in February that year.

18 "White-Collar Criminality," Edwin H. Sutherland, *American Sociological Review* Vol. 5, No. 1 (February, 1940), pp. 1–12.

19 *White-Collar Crime: The Uncut Version*, Edwin H. Sutherland, Yale University Press, 1983, p. 93.

20 The Supreme Court prohibited coercive questioning by 6 votes to 5. Voting in favor of the ban were Gilmar Mendes, Rosa Weber, Dias Toffoli, Ricardo Lewandowski, Marco Aurélio Mello, and Celso de Mello, June 14, 2018.

21 Jean Ziegler, *Os senhores do crime: As novas máfias contra a democracia*. Rio de Janeiro: Record, 2003.

Chapter 6

1 Valmir Moraes da Silva, army lieutenant working as one of the former president's bodyguards.

2 The English version of the Constitution of the Federative Republic of Brazil, Federal Chamber of Deputies. p. 16.

3 From the ruling delivered by Supreme Court judge Gilmar Mendes, suspending former president Lula's appointment as chief of staff. March 18, 2018.

Chapter 7

1 *El País*, "The video in which Emílio Odebrecht says that the scheme has been in place for 30 years and blames the press and Powers," April 17, 2017. Available at: <brasil.elpais.com/ brasil/2017/04/14/politica/149 2192630_931956.html>. Accessed on February 21, 2019.

2 A *Medida Provisória* (Provisional Measure), or *MP*, is an executive act that enables the president to draft legislation and sign it into immediate effect prior to approval by the legislature. It is "provisional" insofar as Congress must pass it into actual law within forty-five days of its publication. It is often seen as a way the executive can temporarily bypass the legislature. Negotiating the approval of MPs with Congress is generally done on a quid-pro-quo basis.

3 The Car Wash task force in Paraná charged the former finance ministers Guido Mantega and Antonio Palocci Filho; former representatives of Odebrecht Marcelo Bahia Odebrecht, Maurício Ferro, Bernardo Gradin, Fernando Migliaccio da Silva, Hilberto Mascarenhas Alves da Silva Filho, and Newton Sergio de Souza; and the marketeers Mônica Regina Cunha Moura, João Cerqueira de Santana Filho, and André Luis Reis de Santana for crimes of active and passive corruption and money laundering. Case: 5033771-51.2018.404.7000. Password: 904895809718. The investigation revealed that Marcelo Odebrecht, aided by Maurício Ferro, Bernardo Gradin, and Newton de Souza, made improper promises to the former finance ministers with a view to having the Provisional Measures passed. Mantega was offered a 50 million real bribe, to be disbursed on request by Fernando Migliaccio and Hilberto da Silva Filho at the Department of Structured Operations. The payment of this bribe led to Provisional Measures 470 and 472, which enabled Braskem (a company in the Odebrecht Group) to parcel its industrialized products tax payments through undue access to credit (PM 420) and granted tax deductions and exemptions for concerns expanding in the North, Northwest, and Midwest of the country (PM 472).

4 One of the main critics of crony capitalism, Schweizer is the author of *Extortion: How Politicians Extract Your Money, Buy Votes and Line Their Own Pockets*. Boston: Mariner Books, 2013.

5 In July 2018, Judge Marcelo Bretas, from the federal courts in Rio, sentenced Eike Batista to thirty years in prison for active corruption and money laundering. He was found guilty of paying bribes to former Rio governor Sérgio Cabral.

6 Chayes, Sarah. *Thieves of the State, Why Corruption Threatens Global Security*, W. W. Norton & Company.

7 Excerpt from Antonio Palocci's plea-bargain testimony, 5026427-19.2018.4.04.7000/PR, event 11, TERMOAUD3, p. 10.

8 According to the *Folha de S.Paulo* newspaper, British government documents show that the Brazilian dictatorship stifled investigations into kickbacks on the purchase of frigates from the UK in the 1970s. For more on this theme, see "Naval relations between the United Kingdom and Brazil during the Cold War: The case of the purchase of the Vosper Frigates," João Roberto Martins Filho, *Brazilian Journal of Strategy & International Relations* e-ISSN 2238-6912 | ISSN 2238-6262| v.4, n. 7, January/June 2015 | pp. 69–97.

9 The full document is available for consultation, in Portuguese, on the public prosecutors' office website: www.mpf.mp.br/para-o-cidadao/caso -lava-jato/entenda-o-caso/ documentos/arquivo-1-regulamento-futebol.

10 Full text available in English at https://www.odebrecht.com/en/ communication/releases/odebrecht-apologizes-its- mistakes.

11 The Lei Áurea (Golden Law) was issued on May 13, 1888, by Isabel, the Princess Imperial of Brazil, officially abolishing slavery in country.

12 Available at https://pdfs.semanticscholar.org.

13 See https://www.theguardian.com/sport/2017/apr/23/brazil-olympic -world-cup-corruption-bribery.

14 The prisoner's dilemma works as follows: two suspects, A and B, are arrested by the police on some minor charge. The cops think they've also committed a more serious crime, but they don't have enough evidence to charge them. So they separate the two and offer both the same deal. If one confesses and testifies against the other, he or she will go free while the other takes the ten-year fall for the crime. If they both refuse to talk, the police will only be able to send them down for six months each on the initial misdemeanor. If both talk, each will be sentenced to five years in jail. This is the dilemma: each prisoner has to decide whether or not to talk but without knowing what his accomplice is planning to do. In the analogy, the prisoners are companies vying for contracts. They are in the dark, not knowing whether to pay bribes or not. As the unilateral decision to pay is always hidden from the other bidders, no company can be sure whether or not its competitors are playing dirty.

15 Susan Rose-Ackerman, Bonnie J. Palifka, *Corruption and Government: Causes, Consequences, and Reform*. Cambridge: Cambridge University Press, 1999.

16 Edwin H. Sutherland, *White Collar Crime, the Uncut Version*, Yale University Press, p. 56.

17 Ibid., p. 99.

18 Ibid, pp. 91–2.

Chapter 8

1 The plea-bargain testimony from Andrade Gutierrez executives concerning corruption on the Maracanã and Metropolitan Ring Road construction jobs provided the bedrock for the charges on which Sérgio Cabral was convicted.

2 Extract from Fernando Cavendish's deposition to Judge Marcelo Bretas at the Rio Federal Court on December 4, 2017.

3 Throughout June 2013, Brazil saw massive street demonstrations nationwide. What started off as a march against a 20-cent rise in bus fare turned into a multi-themed, nonpartisan movement venting general exasperation at the state of the nation. At the movement's peak, close to 2

million people took to the streets across 120 cities and towns throughout the country.

4 Operation Exposed Fracture, launched on April 11, 2017, resulted in both Côrtes and Iskin going to jail. The details of the fraud scheme were revealed by the former undersecretary for health, Cesar Romero.

5 Operation Ratatouille arrested Marco Antônio de Luca on June 1, 2017. He was the owner of a company that paid bribes to state authorities in exchange for contracts with the Rio de Janeiro government.

6 See https://www.independent.co.uk/sport/olympics/rio-olympic-games-2016-governor-2m-lamine-diack- a8989246.html.

7 On October 19, 2017, the federal court accepted an indictment of Cabral and Nuzman on charges of corruption in the purchase of COI votes for the Rio Olympic Games, indicating that public money had been used in the scheme.

8 In his plea-bargain testimony, former vice-president of Caixa Econômica Federal's Government Funds and Lotteries Division, Fábio Cleto, confessed to the receipt of bribes.

9 Fetranspor's payments to Rio lawmakers were revealed in the depositions of no fewer than four figures collaborating with the investigation: the money-mover Álvaro José Novis, who worked for the businessmen; former auditors' court chairman, Jonas Lopes; the owner of the bus company, Marcelo Traça Gonçalves; and Carlos Miranda, Sérgio Cabral's operator.

10 *Source*: Instituto de Segurança Pública (ISP).

11 Jogo do Bicho (Animal Game) was invented in 1892 in Rio de Janeiro by Baron João Batista Viana Drummond, the founder of the Botanical Gardens. It's basically a lottery consisting of a table of twenty-five "houses," each represented by an animal and arranged alphabetically, after the first letter of the animal's name. Each house contains four numbers, from 01 to 04 in the first house, to 97 to 00 in the last. There are many ways the game can be played, but in the simplest versions the player bets on a house/animal, or on a number, say 05 or 62, or on a house and a number—for example, House 25 Vaca (cow) and the number 45. The more complex the bet, the higher the return.

12 Eduardo Campos died in a fatal plane crash on August 13, 2014, in the middle of his campaign for the presidency of Brazil. He was forty-nine years old.

13 Removal of a chief from an investigation under his charge.

Chapter 9

1 In an interview with *O Globo* newspaper on March 11, 2001, Oscar de Barros gave details about how the Cayman Dossier scheme was put together.

2 Letters rogatory, or letters of request, are formal means by which one nation requests legal assistance from another, usually the performance of an act, such as evidence taking, which, if done without sanction, would constitute a violation of sovereignty.

3 Annually updated numbers are available on the Federal Police website: www.pf.gov.br/imprensa/estatistica/operacoes.

4 In 2017, João Santana and Mônica Moura were sentenced to eight years and four months in prison for laundering bribe money paid to PT through kickbacks on contracts with Petrobras. Santana, a political marketing whizz, had been instrumental in the successful electoral campaigns of both Lula and Dilma. These lavish campaigns were largely financed illegally through under-the-table "contributions" from construction company cartels that made billions from padded contracts with the oil giant Petrobras.

5 Temer responded to the fifty questions sent to him by Police Chief Lopes, maintaining his innocence and objecting to what he construed to be the investigator's aggressive tone.

6 Memorandum number 25/2018 was sent by police chiefs from the Supreme Court Investigations Group to the director of the organized crime unit.

Chapter 10

1 Excerpt from the memo sent by the director-general's office to all twenty-seven FP Superintendencies on February 9, 2018.

2 One of the phases of the Rio chapter of Operation Car Wash. The name refers to the 20 percent tax the Portuguese Crown levied on all the gold extracted from Brazil's mines during the Colonial era.

3 In March 2017, the TCE in Rio estimated that kickbacks on the woefully overpriced Maracanã makeover amounted to R$ 211 million.

4 On April 2, 2018, *O Globo* newspaper published a recording of a conversation between the businessman Marcos Andrade Barbosa Silva and advisor Aloysio Neves in which he admits to paying bribes.

5 Contained in Jonas Lopes' plea-bargain testimony.

Chapter 11

1 James Comey, *A Higher Loyalty: Truth, Lies and Leadership*.

2 In his *Diritto e ragione: teoria del garantismo penale*, the Italian legal philosopher Luigi Ferrajoli coined the concept of "*garantismo penale*," which guarantees the citizen's right to trial and freedom to the end of the amplest possible defense. The *garantistas* on the Brazilian Supreme Court

argued that a jail sentence could not begin until after every avenue of appeal had been exhausted. Those arguing in favor of jail time beginning after a conviction upheld by the first appellate court were disdainfully labeled "Punitivists," as if they were hankering for punishment rather than justice. The problem with penal *garantismo* in Brazil is that, in practice, it applies only to those rich enough to carry appeal after appeal, all the way to the Supreme Court, which can take decades in some cases. The concept is particularly contradictory in a country where most of the prison population, poor and underprivileged in their majority, have not even gone to trial yet, much less had convictions upheld at any level. In the case of ex-president Lula, the *punitivistas* originally prevailed by 6 votes to 5, though a second debate on the jurisprudence, held only 579 days later, turned the vote for the *garantistas* by the same margin, and Lula was released from jail.

3 Maluf was initially accused of syphoning R$ 172 million off the construction of a throughway in São Paulo between 1993 and 1996 but was tried only for the embezzlement of R$ 15 million because the statute of limitations had expired on the rest.

4 Available at www1.folha.uol.com.br/poder/2018/04/brasil-possui-ao-menos -58-mil-autoridades-de-40-cargos-com- foro-especial.shtml>. Accessed on: January 15, 2019.

5 According to the federal auditors' court, kickbacks on the refinery's construction were in the order of R$ 2.1 billion.

6 A public/private study conducted in 2019 put "custo Brasil" at R$ 1.5 trillion per year, or 22 percent of GDP.

7 A survey conducted by the digital security firm Avast in 2018 found that 91.8 percent of those interviewed believed the electronic urn system could be tampered with.

Postscript

1 The name Omertà was chosen in allusion to Palocci's code name on the Odebrecht bribery spreadsheets, O Italiano (The Italian), but also in reference to the oath of silence that had prevailed at the construction company until some former staffers at the Department of Structured Operations decided to collaborate with the investigation. Their decision to share what they knew culminated in these search-and-arrest warrants, granted by Judge Sergio Moro only days earlier.

2 In total, the spreadsheet lists eight million reais in payments to Lula. Other important recipients were "Feira," the PT marketeer João Santana (born and raised in Feira de Santana, Bahia), and "Pós Italia" (Post-Italy), former minister Guido Mantega, who replaced Palocci as operator in chief of the corruption scheme.

3 Emílio Odebrecht, Marcelo Odebrecht's father.

4 In the plea-bargain deposition in question, Palocci claimed to have taken
   cash payments directly to Lula at the Air Force Terminal in Brasília,
   where the president would embark on the *Aerolula*. The cash payments
   obtained from Odebrecht—in wads of 30,000–80,000, hidden in cellphone
   or whiskey boxes—were part of the president's four-million reais cut
   in the kickbacks on the construction of the Belo Monte hydroelectric
   mega-dam in the Amazon, considered by many an environmental crime:
   https://www.internationalrivers.org/resources/the-belo-monte-dam-an-
   environmental-crime-7533.

Afterword

1 Individuals jailed on drugs-related crimes account for 28 percent of Brazil's
   prison population. See <www.cnj.jus.br/files/conteudo/arquivo/2017/02
   /b5718a7e7d6f2ede-e274f93861747304.pdf>. Accessed on February 18,
   2019.

ACKNOWLEDGMENTS

Jorge Pontes

First of all, I would like to offer special thanks to my wife, Lilibeth, because her support instilled in me the desire to reinvent myself. This book is for you, in honor of our life together. I thank my mother, Norma, and my father, Jorge M. Pontes (in memoriam), for having given me everything; my children, Beatriz, Vitória, Jorge, Pedro Henrique, and João Guilherme Pontes, for being my reason to look to the future; my close friend Leandro Salles, a constant presence; and my biology teacher, Walter Mello Veiga Silva (in memoriam), for all the life lessons he gave me.

I would also like to thank numerous people who have been important in my career:

The federal agents from the original DMAPH crew: Luena Rego, Mara Fregapani, Cristiane Oioli, and Claudia Bezerra, who left Interpol to help me found the FP's environmental crimes unit and without whom it would never have become the success it did;

The federal agents Angela Mardegan, Cecilia Accioly, Carlos Augusto Abreu, Alvaro Vitor, who were also fundamental in consolidating the fledging unit; the federal agents Sebastião Monteiro, Julio Justo, and Alexandre Finkelstein, for being so productive and professional on our missions to arrest international fugitives;

The federal agents Fabiola Marra, Luciane Marciano, Luís Augusto Maciel, Gilson R. de A. Vasconcelos, Sergio R. Pontes, Eglair Junior, Gustavo Sá, Claudenir Martins, and Ricardo Napoleão, for their friendship and professionalism; the Federal Police chiefs Luis Fernando Almendros, Lacerda Carlos Junior (in memoriam), Jorge de A. Freitas, Alciomar Goersch, Paulo Roberto Ornellas, Valquíria Teixeira, Wilson Damázio, Zulmar Pimentel, Roberto das Chagas Monteiro, José Ercidio Nunes, Roberto Schweitzer, Agílio Monteiro Filho, Getúlio Bezerra, and Paulo Lacerda, my bosses and masters who taught me so much.

The Federal Police chief José Roberto Benedito Pereira, for his assistance with the research;

My fellow police chiefs Marcelo de Oliveira Andrade, Alexandre Saraiva, Vanessa Gonçalves, Paulo de Tarso Teixeira, Luiz Dorea, Rogério Galloro, Geraldo Pereira, Claudia Braga, Tatiana Torres, Delano Bunn, Bernardo Torres, Karla Gomes, Rubens Lopes, Clarissa Cassol, Julia Vergara, Fernando Berbert, Luis Carlos Nóbrega, Fernanda Santos, Fernando Chuy, Adriana Vasconcelos, Denis Cali, Felipe Seixas, Sergio Trivelin, Luis Pontel, Roberto Troncon, Joselio de Sousa, Belmiro Araújo, Carla Patrícia, Renato Cintra, Antônio de Pádua, and Ronaldo Magalhães, who closed ranks with me in the fight against crime; the attaché Philippe Dayer, from Swiss Fedpol, for years of partnership and collaboration;

My friend Judge Denise Frossard, for the example she set and courage she showed in facing organized crime in Rio de Janeiro in the 1990s;

Ambassador Oswaldo Portella, for his support in FP international expansion projects;

The regional public prosecutors Anaiva Oberst, Arthur de Brito Gueiros, Janice Ascari, and Marcelo Ceará Serra Azul, for their partnership and trust;

FBI special agents Richard Ford, Gary Zaugg, James K. Weber, Richard Cavalieros, and Dennis Pierce, for their excellent cooperation over the course of almost two decades;

Under-commissioner of the Polizia di Stato Roberto Donati, for his long-standing friendship and collaboration on joint operations;

Special agent Jill Birchell, from the Fish and Wildlife Service, for her support on so many training programs;

François Lamarque, from the Office National de la Chasse et de la Faune Sauvage, for his indispensable collaboration;

Brigade General of the Gendarmerie Nationale Philippe De Boysere, for invaluable cooperation and friendship;

The police chiefs in Curitiba Erika Marena, Luciano Flores, Igor Romário, and Rosalvo Franco, for harpooning the whale of institutionalized crime and dragging it to the surface like none had ever succeeded in doing before;

The police chiefs and deep-sea fishermen, Cleyber Lopes (chief of the investigation involving president Michel Temer), and Antonio Beabrun (chief of operations on the investigation into ex-governor Sérgio Cabral and his gang) for their help and information;

Professor Robert Rotberg, for the kindness of producing a preface whose quality and sophistication have updated and internationalized our work;

Supreme Court judge Luís Roberto Barroso, for his staunch resistance to institutionalized crime and generosity in penning the afterwords to this book;

The editors Olivia Dellow and Max Vickers, from Bloomsbury, for their professionalism and dedication that made possible to produce the English version our book;

The editors Luíza Côrtes, Marcelo Ferroni, and Bruno Porto, from Grupo Companhia das Letras, for their much-needed support in bringing this book to fruition;

To Federal Judge Sergio Moro, for the example he set at the thirteenth Federal Criminal Court in Curitiba; and last but certainly not least, Márcio Anselmo, coauthor of this book, the police chief who pulled the string that unraveled the yarn that gave rise to Operation Car Wash and whose work has helped change history.

Márcio Anselmo

I'd like to thank Milhomen, Prado, Witt, Macedo, João Paulo, Gabriel, Barth, Luciano, Pace, Renata, Moscardi, Busato, Adriano, Graça, Carbonera, Nitta, Vladimir, Paes, and all the other whalers I have worked with over the years, without whom the facts and events described in the book would certainly never have reached the public.

To the whalers Getúlio Bezerra and Paulo Roberto Falcão Ribeiro, for teaching me to wield the harpoon.

To the police chiefs Erika Marena, Igor Romário, and Rosalvo Ferreira Franco, for believing in my work when it was all just jumbled stacks of paper.

To former judge and Minister of Justice Sergio Fernando Moro, a role model to all in this battle, and to his faithful sidekick Flávia Blanco, always at hand at the most critical times.

To Supreme Court judge Luís Roberto Barroso, steadfast in the trenches of the fight against institutionalized crime, who kindly agreed to write the foreword to Portuguese edition. To Professor Robert Rotberg, for foreword in this English edition.

To Professor Arinda Fernandes, a scholar on the theme of transnational organized crime, for having brought me to the academic life.

To the Professors I have met along the way: Marlene Kempfer, Sandra Lewis, Antenor Madruga, Antonio Cachapuz (in memoriam), Maria Teresa Sadek, Andre Carvalho Ramos, Mark Hamilton, Mirlis Reyes, and so many others.

In short, to all the colleagues I have had the pleasure to work alongside over the last two decades, and who have devoted their careers to the fight against institutionalized crime.

To my partner in this book, Jorge Pontes, for all the hours we shared in devising this project and carrying it forward.

To Grupo Companhia das Letras and the editors Bruno Porto, Marcelo Ferroni, and Luíza Côrtes, for believing in our work. To Bloomsbury Publishing, expecially Max and Olivia, who worked hard on this project.

To all my friends down through the years.

ABOUT THE AUTHORS

Jorge Pontes

Jorge Pontes was born in Rio de Janeiro in 1960. He holds a degree from the University of Amazonas and a Post Degree in Criminal Justice from the University of Virginia, United States, and is a graduate from the FBI National Academy. He spent almost thirty years working for the Federal Police—first as an agent and later as a police chief—both nationwide and abroad, and devoted most of his career to the creation and implementation of units specializing in fighting environmental crime. He was an instructor at the National Police Academy and, in 2006, received the British Parliament Green Apple Award for his operations in the Brazilian Amazon. He was regional superintendent for Pernambuco, coordinator-general and elected member of Interpol's executive committee, and former director of teaching and statistics at the National Public Security Department (Senasp) under the Ministry of Justice.

E-mail: jbpontes@hotmail.com
Instagram: @delegadojorgepontes
Twitter: @JorgeBPontes

Márcio Anselmo

Márcio Anselmo was born in Cambé, Paraná, in 1977 and graduated in law from the State University of Londrina. He joined the Federal Police as a clerk in 2004, stationed in Guaíra, and has since been actively involved in investigating financial crime, corruption, and money laundering. He worked on the Banestado case in Brasília and led the investigations on Operation Faktor, around which time he completed his master's degree. While working on the investigations that gave rise to Operation Car Wash, he studied for a doctorate in international law at the University of São Paulo. From April 2018 to

June 2020, he has occupied the post of coordinator-general of the Corruption and Money Laundering unit. He teaches on postgraduate courses in Brazil and has published various books and papers on organized crime and money laundering. In 2021 he got a Masters Degree in Hemispheric Defense and Security at the Inter-American Defense College (Class 60). He currently lives in Washington D.C. when he has occupied the post of Assistant Research at Inter-American Defense College.

E-mail: maanselmo@gmail.com
Instagram: @delegadomarcioanselmo
Twitter: @delegadomarcio2

INDEX